GĀYATRĪ

The Highest Meditation

ॐ भूर्भुवः स्वः तत्सवितुर्वरेण्यं भर्गो देवस्य
धीमहि धियो योनः प्रचोदयात् ॥
S. SitaRam

GĀYATRĪ

The Highest Meditation

SADGURU SANT KESHAVADAS

MOTILAL BANARSIDASS PUBLISHERS
PRIVATE LIMITED • DELHI

First Edition: New York, 1978
Second Revised Edition: Delhi, 1990
Third Revised Edition: Delhi, 1991
Reprint: Delhi, 1992, 1994

ISBN: 81-208-0697-2

Also available at:

MOTILAL BANARSIDASS

41 U.A. Bungalow Road, Jawahar Nagar, Delhi 110 007
120 Royapettah High Road, Mylapore, Madras 600 004
16 St. Mark's Road, Bangalore 560 001
Ashok Rajpath, Patna 800 004
Chowk, Varanasi 221 001

PRINTED IN INDIA

BY JAINENDRA PRAKASH JAIN AT SHRI JAINENDRA PRESS,
A-45 NARAINA, PHASE I, NEW DELHI 110 028
AND PUBLISHED BY NARENDRA PRAKASH JAIN FOR
MOTILAL BANARSIDASS PUBLISHERS PVT. LTD.,
BUNGALOW ROAD, DELHI 110 007

CONTENTS

SCHEME OF TRANSLITERATION

Vowels		*Consonants*			
अ	a	क	k	त	t
आ	ā	ख	kh	थ	th
इ	i	ग	g	द	d
ई	ī	घ	gh	ध	dh
उ	u	ङ	ṅ	न	n
ऊ	ū	च	c	प	p
ऋ	ṛ	छ	ch	फ	ph
ॠ	ṝ	ज	j	ब	b
ऌ	ḷ	झ	jh	भ	bh
ॡ	ḹ	ञ	ñ	म	m
ए	e	ट	ṭ	य	y
ऐ	ai	ठ	ṭh	र	r
ओ	o	ड	ḍ	ल	l
औ	au	ढ	ḍh	व	v
		ण	ṇ	श	ś
				ष	ṣ
Anusvāra (ं)-ṃ				स	s
Visarga (ः)-ḥ				ह	h

SADGURU SANT KESHAVADAS

INTRODUCTION

SADGURU SANT KESHAVADAS is a spiritual leader of many dimensions. He is also the author of several works. His teachings and writings are like a *Mahā-yāna*, a great ship or vehicle, which is not exclusive, but has a place for everyone, scholars and laymen, Indians and Americans, Hindus and Christians, men and women of all religious persuasions. The present excellent volume on the *Gāyatrī* and its significance and practice truly and fully reflects this universal appeal and approach.

The theme of the work is a most profound one. Lord Kṛṣṇa declares in the *Gītā*: "Among the various forms of worship and sacrifice, I am *japa*—meditation." Thus, God dwells in the *japa*. "By *japa* alone", the great law-giver and prophet Manu says: "A spiritual person will undoubtedly attain bliss and ultimate fulfilment. It is immaterial if he performs or omits to perform other sacred rituals. Such a spiritual person is the true friend of the world" (*Manu-smṛti* II.87).

Japa is the constant repetition of a mantra, accompanied by an intense meditation on the deity invoked by the mantra. *Gāyatrī* is declared to be the highest mantra in Hindu religious writings. It is the very essence of the three holy *Veda*-s, *Ṛk*, *Yajus* and *Sāman*. "Brahmā, the Supreme Creator, drew out each one of the three *pādas* of this mantra from each one of the three *Veda*-s" (*Manu-smṛti* II.77).

The Supreme Deity invoked by the *Gāyatrī*-mantra is the Light symbolized by the physical luminary, the sun. There is an ancient symbol of Christ as the Solar Christ, Christ symbolized by the sun. Not only is physical solar energy highly beneficial to mankind in providing heat, as we are now more aware, but it also stimulates and nourishes all life and heals various diseases. The ineffable, resplendent Supreme Reality, the Light behind the sun, is a source of unsurpassed spiritual energy, upon which, by the repetition of *Gāyatrī* and its meditation, mankind can draw forth stimulation and nourishment of the higher intellect and ultimate spiritual fulfilment.

Gāyatrī helps the higher man to be born in all of us. She is the "Savior of the singer of the mantra." *Gāyatrī* is the only mantra whose name ends in *tra* (meaning protection, saving force, and grace).

This book on *Gāyatrī* by Sant Keshavadas, joyfully performs several functions. It, of course, beautifully explains the central meaning and significance of the mantra in all its fullness. But, it also describes such practical things as the use of purificatory water rites and the techniques of this *japa*: posture of sitting, time, atmosphere, proper breath control, the use of the fingers of the hand for the various *kriyā*-s, the use of rosary, the proper pronunciation of the sacred sounds, etc. This will immensely help the new practitioner and will educate and put him on the path of practice.

The volume also discusses the hidden meanings of the *Praṇava* and the *Vyāhṛti* portions of the mantra. There is a highly useful chart at the end which indicates the seven-fold symbolism of the *Vyāhṛti* and relates and integrates it with the seven-fold aspects of the macrocosm and the microcosm and the aspects of life. If the *Gāyatrī*-mantra is understood, repeated, and meditated upon, in the manner so completely described and explained in this rare and unusual volume, it will be productive of the highest bliss, unparalleled intellect and creativity, and manifold mastery and success in the world.

We owe deep gratitude to Sant Keshavadas for this outstanding book on *Gāyatrī*, which fulfils a need in this important field and subject area for the readers. Also, we are deeply grateful to Dr. Shyam Argade and Mrs. Veena Argade, for their unique benefaction and loving munificence, without which the printing and publication of this book would not have been possible. Dr. Argade's father has performed *Gāyatrī* meditation several million times in his life. Veena and Shyam have shown great devotion, dedication, and leadership in the promotion of various causes and in the religious and cultural life of the Indian community of Greater Detroit. They are also devoted and loving disciples of Sadguru Sant Keshavadas. May the Supreme Mother Gāyatrī, the holy *tattvārtha-varṇātmika*, confer Her manifold blessings upon them and their children and family.

T.K. VENKATESWARAN
Professor, Department of Religious Studies
University of Detroit

PREFACE

THERE IS NO greater meditation than *Gāyatrī* meditation. There are very few books available on this profound subject in English. With the material available in Sanskrit and other languages an humble attempt is made to describe the many facets of this most ancient meditation.

The sages of the Himalayas have demonstrated to the world at large that one can live a long life with perfect health by meditating on *Gāyatrī*-mantra. All the masters of yore and the living masters constantly meditate on this mantra and have made it a rule for all those who follow the path of *Veda*-s or revelations to practise *Sandhyā-vandana* or meditation on Father-Mother God through the light of the sun. As the whole humanity in its evolutionary process must reach the Light of Truth and attain immortality, the best and the highest meditation is presented here by giving reverence to the tradition but still explaining it to the modern man.

One may have to read this book very carefully, reverentially, and many times before one can really understand fully the contents. It is just impossible to simplify them more than what has been done here.

I have had assistance from several people so that this book could see the light of the day. First of all, I want to thank my spiritual disciples of the Temple of Cosmic Religion, Southfield, Michigan, for their continuous cooperation. May God bless Sri Ravidas, Sri Chandrashekhar, and Sister Karuna. My special blessings go to Sister Karuna for her dedicated service in typing, editing, and doing everything needed to bring this book together. May God bless her with greater energy and health for helping me to write more books. May the Universal Mother bless Narayanadas of Michigan for the wonderful artwork of

Gāyatrīdevī included in this book. I am grateful to Dr. Shyam Argade and his devoted wife, Smt. Veena Argade, for their kind donation that made the printing of this book possible. May Gāyatrīdevī bless them and their children with prosperity and peace.

I must also thank my dear Rand Martin Holiday for his timely help in making the publication of this book possible. It is my joyful duty to thank my beloved friend, Professor Sri T.K. Venkateswaran, Chairman, Department of Religious Studies, University of Detroit, for his most profound Introduction to this holy book. May Goddess Gāyatrī bless him, his family, and children.

Finally, I pray to the Divine Mother Gāyatrī to bless all who read this book with health, prosperity, and peace. May the entire world be filled with peace! Om and Prem

February 28, 1977 SANT KESHAVADAS
Southfield, Michigan

GĀYATRĪ-SĀDHANĀ

From the book *Sādhanā*
by Śrī Swāmī Śivānanda

Philosophy of Gāyatrī-sādhanā

Of all mantra-s, the supreme and the most potent power of powers is the great, glorious *Gāyatrī*-mantra.

It is the support of every seeker after Truth who believes in its efficacy, power and glory, be he of any caste, creed, clime, or sect. It is only one's faith and purity of heart that really count. Indeed, *Gāyatrī* is an impregnable spiritual armour, a veritable fortress, that guards and protects its votary, that transforms him into the divine, and blesses him with the brilliant light of the highest spiritual illumination. Whatever your *Iṣṭa-devatā* may be, the regular repetition of a few *mālā*-s of *Gāyatrī* every day will bestow upon you all that is auspicious and benevolent, herein and hereafter.

It is wrong to conceive of the notion that *Gāyatrī* is solely meant for the chosen orthodox *brahmin* class. It is universally applicable, for it is nothing but an earnest prayer for Light, addressed to the Almighty Supreme Spirit. It is verily the sole transcendental guide-light to humanity. This is the greatest of all mantra-s and its presiding deity is the *Parabrahman* Itself. Yet it is acceptable to all types of aspirants, for it is conceived as worship of *Devī*, of *Lord Hari*, of *Āditya* or the sun, and also as pure *Nirguṇa* worship of *Brahman*.

The *Tejas* of the *brahmacārī* (celibate) lies in his *Gāyatrī-japa*. The support and prosperity of the *Gṛhastha* (householder) is again the *Gāyatrī*; strength and solace of the *Vānaprastha* (recluse) is again the *Gāyatrī*. Thus, from the moment of the young student's *Upanayanam* (investiture with the sacred thread), until the moment when he enters the glorious state of *Sannyāsa* (monkhood), throughout his life the *Gāyatrī*-mantra is his constant guide, support, and strength. To him, the *Gāyatrī*-mantra is the *summum bonum* of life.

If you start regular daily *Gāyatrī-japa* you will feel the wondrous power that you derive from it. Fix a particular time for the *japa* and stick to it permanently. At least one *mālā* of *japa* must be done daily without break. It will guard you from all dangers, give you infinite strength to overcome all obstacles, and take you to the very pinnacle of splendour, power, peace, and bliss.

Practice of Gāyatrī-sādhanā

Brahmā milked out, as it were, from the three *Vedas*, the letter *A*, the letter *U*, and the letter *M*, and formed by their coalition three triliteral monosyllables, together with three mysterious words—*Bhūr*, *Bhuvaḥ* and *Svaḥ*, or earth, sky, and heaven. From the three *Veda*-s also the Lord of creatures incomprehensibly exalted and successfully milked out the three measures of that ineffable text, beginning with the word *Tat* and entitled *Sāvitrī* or *Gāyatrī* (*Manu-smṛti,* II.76-77).

Thus came:

Oṃ Bhūr Bhuvaḥ Svaḥ;
Tat Savitur vareṇyaṃ bhargo devasya dhīmahi;
Dhiyo yo naḥ pracodayāt.

Let us meditate on *Īśvara* and His glory, who has created the universe, who is fit to be worshipped, who is the remover of all sins and ignorance. May He enlighten our intellect.

The Lord says in the *Veda*-s "*samāno mantraḥ*", let one *mantra* be common to all, and the *mantra* is the *Gāyatrī.* The secret lore of the *Upaniṣad*-s is that essence of the four *Veda*-s, while the *Gāyatrī* with the three *vyāhṛti*-s is the essence of the *Upaniṣad*-s.

Gāyatrī is the mother of the *Veda*-s and the destroyer of all sins. The monosyllable *Oṃ* is an emblem of the Supreme. There is nothing more purifying on earth than the *Gāyatrī*. The *japa* of *Gāyatrī* brings the same fruit as the recitation of all the *Veda*-s with the *Aṅga*-s. This single mantra, repeated sincerely and with clear conscience, brings the supreme good.

PRAYER TO GĀYATRĪ

Yā sandhyāmaṇḍalagatā yā trimūrti-svarūpiṇī/
Sarasvatī yā Sāvitrī tām vande veda-mātaram//

The Goddess in the solar orb, who is of the form of the Trinity, who is both Sarasvatī and Sāvitrī—I bow to (that Gāyatrī), Mother of the Veda-s.

Yā viśva-jananī devī yā trimūrti-svarūpiṇī/
Gāyatrī-rūpiṇī yā hi tām vande sapta-mātṛkām//

The Goddess who is the Mother of the worlds, who is of the form of the Trinity and who is of the form of Gāyatrī—I bow to that form of the Seven Mothers.

PART I

Mantra-yoga

YOGA

YOGA IS UNION with God. Yoga is also the pathway to God, which finally results in such union. There are many Yogas, but four are chosen mainly for Self-realization. These are *Jñāna*-yoga, *Karma*-yoga, *Bhakti*-yoga, and *Rāja*-yoga. Strictly speaking, the first three are considered paths for God-realization in the *Bhagavad-gītā*, the fourth only preparing the psychological field for such realization. All of these Yoga-s are complementary to each other and are never contradictory, even though they begin with different roads.

Intellect, will, and emotion are the ruling factors in a human being. Intellect leads to knowledge, will leads to selflessness, and emotion leads to love. For knowledge to become wisdom, it should be backed by love; for love to become divine, it should be guided by wisdom. Both should lead our will towards selfless service.

Rāja-yoga aims at all the above by its eight limbs or *aṣṭāṅga*. Thus perfecting the instruments in us by the technique of Yoga, we march to the highest realms of consciousness to merge in God.

Chanting, singing, and *kīrtana* are used mainly in *Bhakti*-yoga, even though other Yoga-s also employ them for concentration or meditation on God. *Bhakti*-yoga is a big tree of various branches, of which the main branches are *Mantra*-yoga, union with the Truth through chanting mantra-s; *Nāda*-yoga, realizing God through sounds or music; and *Kīrtana*-Yoga, praising God through songs, dance, and explaining His glories through stories with their esoteric teachings, which is the major branch of *Bhakti*, for it includes chanting and music, devotion and meditation.

MANTRA-YOGA

IN REGARD TO the chanting of mantra-s or *Mantra*-yoga, what is a mantra? Mantra is a powerful word or a combination of words heard by a sage. Mantra is that word which takes the man who sincerely chants it across the ocean of rebirth. This is the highest meaning of the term 'mantra'. There are other lesser meanings also. Mantra is an occult formula to remove various troubles or to fulfil various mundane desires, depending upon the motives with which the mantra-s are chanted. Mantra is an incantation which, when uttered with correct intonation, yields results through the forces of nature, deities, or angels whom one propitiates, whose hymn one utters or chants. Mantra is a word-power which could be used for spiritual realization or material desires; it could be utilized for one's own welfare or destruction. It is like atomic energy. It is a power, acting according to the devotion of the man who uses it.

Mantra-vidyā is really the science of thought. The world has come from the thought of God. It emerged into gross form by the projection of His word *Oṃ*. *Oṃ* is Veda or knowledge of God. It is *nāda* or sound. Thus one can see that mantra, *nāda* and *Veda* are all inter-linked. The Veda-s are full of mantra-s of great thought-powers which have come from *nāda* or sound. Thus, every mantra has a particular *nāda* or sound intonation. If the intonation is not known, the mantra may not yield the full result. Therefore, students of the Veda-s know that mantra-s of the *Ṛg-veda* are chanted differently from the mantra-s of the *Sāma-veda*. At the same time, it is not enough to know only the sounds, but one should also know the words, without which the results will not be the same. There are examples in the Veda-s where opposite results occurred for failure to utter the words of the mantra correctly.

Therefore, Mantra-vidyā or Mantra-yoga is a great thought-science which should be practised under a competent teacher.

Mantra-yoga's proper use is elevating. Its misuse is dangerous. Such a powerful word or mantra can express itself either as a written or spoken word. The written word or *Varṇātmaka-śabda*, contains syllables, words, or sentences, whereas the spoken word or *dhvanyātmaka-śabda* is *nāda* or manifestation of thought through certain sounds. It could be either mere sounds or words spoken, chanted, or sung. Each type is used according to the necessity, capacity, and motive of the practitioner. *Nāda-brahma* or Sound-brahma is heard in *anāhata-cakra* or the heart's centre. Mystics hear the voice of God from this *cakra*. The *ṛṣi*-s have recognized thirty-three species (*koṭi*) or thirty-three crores, i.e. 330 million *devatā*-s or divine beings of various gradations, who have their abodes in various *loka*-s or spheres. Each *devatā* or celestial being has a name or mantra for which he is the presiding deity. Therefore, when one chants certain mantra-s, certain *devatā-s* are invoked and they respond according to the intensity of the meditation. If you receive a mantra of a *devatā* or deity from a guru and sincerely practise that mantra with worship and meditation, that deity will appear before you, either physically or in your meditation, to fulfil your desires. The mind, occupied in contemplation of such a deity, takes the shape of that deity or becomes as powerful and pure as that deity. Through the mantra you can please the *devatā*, who will fulfil your desires.

In order to propitiate a deity, *mantra-kriyā* (action in the form of worship, either external or internal), and *bhakti* (devotion) are essential. If a man chants a mantra without *bhakti* or devotion, it becomes mechanical and the deity will not be pleased. Or, if a man chants or meditates upon the mantra devotionally but offers neither external form of worship with knowledge of its esoteric meaning nor internal worship, such as sacrificing the ego or burning all desires, etc., then also the result will not be complete. But when *mantra-kriyā*, and *bhakti* are all combined, the result is beneficial. Therefore, after chanting, meditating, or worshipping, the practitioner should pray: "God, all that I have done has been done in an imperfect way. Be pleased with my devotion and pour Thy grace upon me." This was the method of the ancient seers.

God will forgive the seeker for his imperfections, for He is pleased even with a guileless heart but with devotion and will bestow boons upon such a devotee. Thus, mantra without *bhakti* and *kriyā* will not yield results.

VARIETIES OF MANTRA-S

THERE ARE various kinds of mantra-s. They can be broadly divided into Vedic mantra-s, *Tāntrika* mantra-s, and *Purāṇic* mantra-s. Again, each one of these is further divided into *sāttvika*, *rājasika*, and *tāmasika* mantra-s. Mantra-s which are chanted for illumination, light, wisdom, supreme divine love, compassion, and realization of God are *sāttvika* mantra-s. Those chanted for progeny and worldly prosperity are *rājasika* mantra-s, and those chanted to propitiate evil spirits in order to destroy or harm others or for vicious deeds are *tāmasika* mantra-s. Among these, the last is sinful and such intent is called *vāma-mārga*, or black-magic. *Rājasika* mantra-s will give worldly success and prosperity but in order to enjoy the result of this good karma, men are born again and again. The *sāttvika* mantra-s, however, destroy all karma and lead to final beatitude after death and tranquillity and equanimity while living.

THREE LIMBS OF MANTRA

MANTRA IS the sacred word with power. It could be divided into three sections:

1. Mantra which is a thought-power given in a few syllables or words for meditation by a guru.

2. *Stotra* or prayer to a deity which may be subdivided into (a) general or (b) specific. General *stotra*-s are for general goodness that has to come from God according to His will. Specific prayers are prayers of an individual to God to fulfil some of his specific desires.

3. *Kavaca* or mantra-s used as an armour for protection. Many great *kavaca*-s or mantra-armours are found in the great epics and Purāṇa-s of India. Thus, mantra, *stotra*, and *kavaca* are the three limbs of the *mantra-devatā* or the deity that presides over a mantra. One who knows this secret and follows the discipline reaches the goal.

ṢOḌAŚOPACĀRA OR SIXTEEN STEPS OF WORSHIP

In Mantra-yoga there are sixteen steps of worship of the image or symbol of the deity and meditation on a particular aspect of the deity which one wants to propitiate. The sixteen steps of worship are:

1. *Āvāhana*, invoking God.
2. *Āsana* (Here it means welcoming God to take His seat in the image or the symbol which we worship); esoterically, it is the offering of one's heart as the throne or seat.
3. *Pādya*, washing the feet of the symbol. Here the water offered is devotion to the feet of God.
4. *Arghya*, the offering of water to the hands of God, is offering oneself to the hands of God.
5. *Ācamana*, offering pure water for sipping.
6. *Snāna*, ceremonial bathing with milk, sugar, honey, and water.
7. *Vastra* is the offering of new and beautiful clothes and wrapping them around the image. This means donning oneself with divine wisdom and living in the world untainted by passion.
8. *Upavīta*, the offering of the sacred thread, which means to be filled with pure thoughts.
9. *Vilepana* is besmearing the supraphysical body of God with musk, red powder, and sandalwood paste. This means adorning the Lord with all that is noble in man.
10. *Puṣpa* is offering flowers, which means offering our heart.
11. *Dhūpa* is the burning of incense, which is really the burning of sins by the fire of wisdom.

12. *Dīpa* is the wick light, which is kept or waved before the holy symbol of God. This is the act of burning the egoistic mind and karma.
13. *Naivedya* is the offering of food, which is offering of great mantra-s or prayers.
    A. *Tāmbūla* is the offering of betal leaf and betal nut to purify the mouth after food. This is the word of wisdom emanating from the feast of mantra.
    B. *Jala* is the water to rinse one's mouth, which means the subtle desires (*vāsanā*-s) are also thrown out by rinsing.
    C. *Madhuparka* is the fruit offered after the rinsing of the mouth. Fruits are the four types of liberation called *sārūpya*, or attaining the likeness of God; *sālokya*, or living in the abode of God; *sāmīpya*, or living near God; and *sāyujya*, or merging in God.
14. *Pradakṣiṇa-namaskāra*, perambulation and salutation.
15. *Mantrapuṣpa*, offering flowers and red rice for world peace.
16. *Śayyā* is the offering of the most beautiful bed to God to rest. It means offering our pure heart to God and praying to Him to make our heart His abode.

These sixteen steps are described as *Ṣoḍaśopacāra-pūjā* or sixteen steps of mantra worship offered to God.

JAPA-YOGA

THE UNIVERSE emerged from the indestructible sound. It is the vibration of the sound which has projected this universe. Thus, universe is controlled by sound. Whosoever controls this sound can control the universe. The Cosmic Mind is propitiated by sound. But it is a definite thought formula and it has intonation. This thought formula is called the mantra. It releases its power and reveals its truth to those who meditate on it repeatedly. This repetition of the holy incantation of the mantra is what is called *japa*.

In the *Bhagavad-gītā*, Lord Kṛṣṇa says, "Among *yajña*-s I am the *Japa-yajña*." *Yajña* means sacrifice. The whole universe and Truth are established in *yajña*. There is the *Vidhi-yajña* which is ritualistic sacrifice; munificent gift which is *Dravya-yajña*; imparting of wisdom which is *Jñāna-yajña*; and various austerities through which Truth is realized is *Tapa-yajña*. Even though there are so many *yajña*-s, how is it that Lord Kṛṣṇa gave importance to *Japa-yajña*? The reason according to *Liṅga Purāṇa* is that in all the other *yajña*-s some sort of injury is involved. *Japa-yajña* alone is pure and simple, especially when the repetition of the mantra is mental—hence its glory. Secondly, the purpose of all *yajña*-s is the realization of God. But most of the *yajña*-s are performed for obtaining worldly or heavenly happiness; thus, it is for fulfilment of the desires. But the purpose of yoga is desirelessness and the attainment of enlightenment, which is attained successfully in mental repetition or repeated meditation on the mantra.

The definition of *japa* according to *Agni Purāṇa* runs thus:

The syllable '*ja*' destroys the birth and death cycle and the syllable '*pa*' destroys all the sins. Thus that which destroys all the sins and puts an end to the birth-death cycle and liberates souls from the bondage is *japa*.

There are two forms of *japa*. One is the *Vācika* or oral, another is *Mānasika* or mental. In *Vācika*, there are two divisions. One is *Upāṃśu* where the mantra is repeated with the movement of the lips without making any sound. The other division is oral where movement of the lips is accompanied with sound. In mental *japa*, there are two methods. One is mental repetition; another is the meditation on the breath which is called *Ajapa-japa*. *Vācika* or oral *japa* is defined thus: "When the mantra is uttered very clearly within the hearing of others, it is called oral *japa*." And, "when the man who repeats alone hears and even the one who is sitting very near hears not, when the lips alone are moving, such *japa* is called *Upāṃśu*."

The mental repetition is described thus: "Meditation on the spirit of the mantra and the meaning of the sacred word, without movement of the tongue or the lips, is *Mānasika* or mental *japa*." Among the various methods of repetition of mantra, this type of mental repetition is considered the highest. Manu declares: "The oral *japa* is ten times more meritorious than the ritualistic sacrifice. *Upāṃśu-japa* is a hundred times better and the mental *japa* is a thousand times greater."

For a beginner, mental *japa* is very difficult. It requires the following. For the destruction of *tamo-guṇa*, or inertia, one should repeat loudly or have the *Vācika-japa*. To purify *rajo-guṇa*, or passion, one should cultivate *Upāṃśu*. He whose mind is tranquil or filled with *sattva-guṇa* alone becomes fit to have the *Mānasika* or mental *japa*. Of course, a man who has attained perfection could use anyone of the methods to teach humanity, but for beginners these disciplines were taught.

Japa-yajña cannot be compared with any other form of sacrifice. The other sacrifices and the rituals in which pouring of oblations is mainly observed, like the *Jyotiṣṭoma* or *Rājasūya,* have only one-sixteenth of the merit of *Japa-yajña* in the opinion of Manu. Mergence in the thought-power is one of the great characteristics of *japa*.

In *Liṅga Purāṇa*, Śiva says to his dazzling spouse, Pārvatī: "Devi, in all the other *yajña*-s, some form of injury is done either through thought, word, or deed, but in *Japa-yajña*, there is no such injury. That is why the *Japa-yajña* is greatest of all." Semi-gods, demons, goblins, fiends, and ghosts cannot approach or come near the man who repeats the holy mantra-s. *Japa* destroys the accumulated storage of actions; it bestows all happiness and delivers one from bondage and brings salvation.

SIGNIFICANCE OF ENVIRONMENT IN JAPA

ACCORDING TO *Tantrasāra*, "mental *japa* could be done in any place at all times." *Liṅga Purāṇa* gives a great significance to certain environments which bring more merit than any other place. It says:

> When you do *japa* in your home, the merit will be only as much as the count of *japa*; whereas, if chanted in a cow pen, the merit is hundredfold greater. If the same *japa* is done on the bank of a holy river, the merit will be a hundred thousand more than the previous two. If the same *japa* is done in front of the holy image of God, its merit could never be counted. On the shores of an ocean, on mountains, in temples, hermitages, the *japa* brings untold merits. The *japa* done in front of Lord's image or gazing at the pole star and the sun-god are very efficacious. The *japa* done in front of a flame, fire, and cow are meritorious; likewise, the holy mantra and *japa* done in front of the guru, the spiritual preceptor.

It is said in the *Tantrasāra* that the *japa* done in the garden of *Tulasī*, *i.e.* among the basil plants, or the *Bilva* trees that are dear to Śiva, or among the holy fig trees at the top of a mountain, on the bank of a river, in a cow pen, in the temple surroundings, in pilgrimage centres, or in the presence of the guru, controls the mind very easily and the repetition of the mantra shall certainly bring perfection and the attainment of spiritual joy.

THE ROSARY IN JAPA

JUST AS THE efficacy of the environment is important in *japa*, similarly the various powers of various types of beads are described. *Tantrasāra* describes:

> Counting the *japa* through the fingers by the tip of the thumb is eight-fold; the beads prepared from the seed of a holy tree called *Putrajīva* brings tenfold merit. The beads prepared from the conch-shell bring hundredfold; that which is counted by the beads prepared from the shiny stones brings thousand-fold merit; the beads made up of jewels, if used to count, bring ten-thousandfold merit. Crystal beads are also similar whereas pearl beads bring a hundred-thousandfold merit. And the rosary of lotus beads is ten times more than the previous one. The gold rosary brings millionfold merit. More than all these, knots of the *Kuśa* grass, *Tulasī* beads, and the holy *Rudrākṣa* bring infinite results.

Worshippers of Viṣṇu use the rosary of the *Tulasī* beads. For worshippers of Gaṇeśa, the rosary of beads prepared from the tusk of an elephant is auspicious. Worshippers of Goddess Kālī and Śiva use sandalwood beads or *Rudrākṣa*.

In *Kālikā Purāṇa*, for the fulfilment of desires, certain rosaries are considered auspicious. The rosary of *Kuśa* beads is considered the destroyer of all sins. The rosary of *Putrajīva* beads bestows children; and the rosary of crystals fulfils all desires. Coral brings wealth. It is clearly stated that the same rosary should not contain all sorts of beads.

In *Sanatkumāra Saṃhitā*, the thread and the colour over which the beads are woven are also stated. Cotton thread fulfils four types of pursuit. They are *Dharma* (Law Divine), *Artha* (prosperity), *Kāma* (desire and enjoyment), and *Mokṣa* (liberation). White thread is to gain peace; red is to attract people; yellow is for selfish purposes; and black is for wealth, worldly and spiritual. Sometimes the colour is selected according to the order in society. Thus white thread is for the *Brahmins* (priests), yellow for the warrior class, and black for business people. Red thread for a rosary is for all the four *varṇa*-s or orders in society.

The *mālā* (rosary) should look like the cowtail or like a coiled serpent. It has to be purified by the sacred combination of five liquids, viz., milk, honey, curd, sugar, and water called *Pañcagavya.* The guru, purifying the *mālā*, chants the holy mantra called *Sadyojāta-mantra. Sadyojāta* is a mantra which gives a new birth into spiritual life. Therefore, it is prayed to bring salvation to the chanter. Then the rosary is worshipped by invoking creative energy into it. In *Vārāhi Tantra*, the mantra to invoke Devī is stated:

> O Divine Rosary, you are of the form of all wisdom. You confer on me all joy and peace here and hereafter and bless me to attain perfection.

In another great book called *Yoginīhṛdaya*, the prayer to the rosary is stated thus:

> O Divine Rosary, you are bringing me the blessings of all the gods. By your Power I shall attain the Truth. O Mother, to Thee I make obeisance.

With such a great reverence, the rosary should be worshipped and used in repeating the holy mantra.

In case the rosary falls down or breaks, it is considered inauspicious. Then one has to chant "*Hrīṃ*" to purify the *mālā* and chant 108 times the holy name of God.

Sit in lotus posture or free lotus posture. Hold the *mālā* in your right hand, hanging it over the three fingers, the middle finger, ring finger, and the little finger. Count the beads by pushing them one by one by the thumb and the middle finger, but, as a rule, the index finger is avoided in *japa*. The reason is that the index represents the individual ego which differentiates; so the scriptures say that the index is avoided during *japa*. When you have finished your japa 108 times, do not cross the *Meru*-bead (the big bead distinguished from all the other beads); instead, reverse the counting to complete your *sādhanā*. Mantra and bead counting should go together until you have transcended body consciousness, where you make the breaths or the thoughts of the mind themselves the beads. May God bless you so that you may reach the summit of experience in this very life through spiritual *sādhanā*!

PREPARATION

ONE SHOULD have a separate worship or meditation room. A photo, image, or symbol of the chosen deity (*Iṣṭa-devatā*) or of the great masters and gurus should be placed there. Flowers and incense create the atmosphere. The room should be simple and clean and should not be used for any other purpose except worship and meditation. After bathing or washing one's limbs and face, one should enter the meditation room. The rosary of *Tulasī* or *Rudrākṣa* or any holy beads will be very helpful for *japa* or the repetition of the holy mantra. Sitting in the lotus posture or any easy posture, holding the back, chest, and chin straight, one should gaze at the symbol, image, or light and then close one's eyes and meditate on it. Sit on a deerskin or tiger skin. Skin is auspicious because it severs one from the earth's vibrations and disturbances. When they are not available, one could use a thick cloth to sit upon.

Gazing in between the eyebrows or at the tip of the nose is also practised by yogī-s. One could close the eyes and meditate in between the eyebrows (*Bhrū-madhya*), or the heart's lotus (*Hṛt-padma*), or the thousand-petalled lotus (*Sahasrāra-cakra*). One could meditate on light (*jyoti*) or on sound (*nāda*). A little breathing exercise before beginning, and again on closing the meditation, is very healthy. To prepare the mind for such concentration, one could read certain verses from the holy scriptures or one could sing the divine names of God or songs of saints, which elevate the mind and make one enter into meditation.

PRAYER OR KĪRTANA

THERE ARE many prayer mantra-s or hymns praising God which are very powerful, sometimes more powerful than meditation, because they make God with attributes appear before you or you may have a mystic vision of your personal God. In such cases, it is not prayers or *kīrtana* that lead toward meditation but rather that meditation has become a means for such spontaneous flow of *kīrtana* which brings the direct perception of Reality. It is only prayerful meditation that makes one realize God. Prayer springs from the heart. Meditation without prayer may lead to sloth and sleep just as prayer without meditation may become mere lip service. Then there are prayers or *kīrtana*-s which emerge when one is face to face with God. Such prayers are very powerful and could move the entire world. It is such hymns which have emerged from the hearts of seers or saints after the rich experience of the perception of God that one finds in the *Veda*-s.

For example, the greatest of all the mantras is *Gāyatrī*, a prayer which was revealed to Sage Viśvāmitra after a transcendental experience in meditation. Such prayers are "whispers of cosmic consciousness". All the *Upaniṣad*-s begin and end with a prayer. If there is a prayer before meditation, then there is a prayer after meditation. For example, "Lead us from untruth toward the Truth; from darkness toward the Light; from death toward immortality", is the greatest prayer mantra. It is invariably chanted by all the sages. It is a universal mantra. Silent prayer is meditation; meditational song is prayer.

WHAT IS AUṂ?
(*Pronounced "Oṃ"*)

THIS IS THE Primal Sound. This is the name of *Brahman* or God. *Auṃ* stands for Brahmā the creator, Viṣṇu the preserver, and Śiva the destroyer. It stands for the whole universe made up of *triguṇa*-s or the triple manifestations of nature. They are *sattva-guṇa* or tranquillity, *rajoguṇa* or passionate activity, and *tamo-guṇa*, inactivity. Esoterically, *Auṃ* stands for our physical, astral, and causal bodies, and indicates *Ātmā* which is beyond the three. *A* is gutteral, *U* is middle, and *M* is the labial or end of the vocal chord. In short, *Auṃ* stands for all that is manifested and un-manifested. It is the word from which everything has come. It is the *Nāda-Brahma* or Sound-Brahma. It is the *bīja* or seed mantra and is usually prefixed to all the other mantras. The heart is the seat of *Ātmā* and from the heart spring one hundred and eight *nāḍī*-s. So, it is interesting to note that the minimum number of mantra-s to be chanted is one hundred and eight. Therefore, the beads on a rosary are generally one hundred and eight in number.

Oṃ is the Eternal; *Oṃ* is all this universe. *Oṃ* is the syllable of assent. Saying "*Oṃ*! Let us hear", they begin the citation. With *Oṃ*, they sing the hymns of the *Sāma Veda*. With "*Oṃ Shom*", they pronounced the *śāstra*-s. With *Oṃ*, the priest officiating at the sacrifice says the response. With *Oṃ*, Brahmā begins creation. With *Oṃ*, one sanctions the burnt offerings. With *Oṃ*, the Brahmin, ere he expounds the knowledge, cries, "May I attain the Eternal. Verily he attains" (*Taittirīya Upaniṣad*, Chapter 8).

Oṃ is Brahmā. *Oṃ* is the word of *Brahmā*. *Oṃ* is Sound-Brahman (*Śabda-Brahman*). *Oṃ* is the sound which projected the universe. During cosmic dissolution, the universe merged in *Oṃ*. *Oṃ* has no beginning. *Oṃ* has no end. *Oṃ* was before time was created. *Oṃ* is beyond time, space, and causation. *Oṃ* is beyond past, present, and future. *Oṃ* is beyond nether, earth, and ethereal regions. *Oṃ* is beyond *sattva* (brilliance), *rajas* (passion), and *tamas* (darkness). *Oṃ* is beyond Brahmā the creator, Viṣṇu the preserver, and Śiva the destroyer. *Oṃ* is Supreme (*Parātparaḥ*).

Oṃ moves the *prāṇa* or the cosmic vital force. In man, *Oṃ* is expressed through *prāṇavāyu* or the vital breath. Hence it is called *praṇava*. In man, *Oṃ* is beyond the gross, subtle, and the causal bodies. It is beyond wakeful, dream, and deep sleep states of consciousness. In every breath, man utters it, repeats it unintentionally and inevitably. Every vibration in the body and in the universe emerges from *Oṃ*, is sustained in *Oṃ*, and returns to *Oṃ*. Every humming emerges from *Oṃ*. A child cries, "*Oṃ*, *Oṃ*"; musicians hum, "*Oṃ*, *Oṃ*"; bees buzz, "*Oṃ*, *Oṃ*"; the ocean roars, "*Oṃ*, *Oṃ*". To aching man, humming soothes; to ailing man, *Oṃ* cures; to poets, it brings inspiration. To the philosopher, it brings realization. *Oṃ* is the consent of man for God to enter into him. *Oṃ* is the expression of the seer of Truth. *Oṃ* is Veda, the wisdom of God. *Oṃ* is the *nāda*, the sound of God. *Oṃ* is eternal, the indestructible word. *Oṃ* is the nectar in God-Soul union cord.

Oṃ is the one quest of all the saints. *Oṃ* is the one search of all sages. *Oṃ* is the one search of all the sciences. *Oṃ* is the one goal of all the souls. *Oṃ* is the One Truth which is worshipped in diverse ways.

Oṃ brings equilibrium. *Oṃ* brings wisdom. *Oṃ* is the root. *Oṃ* is the support. *Oṃ* pervades all. *Oṃ* sustains all. *Oṃ* brings peace, bliss, and power. *Oṃ* kills the ego, desires, and doubt. *Oṃ* is the abode of the soul. *Oṃ* is the language of God. *Oṃ* is expressed by God, *Oṃ* expresses God, *Oṃ* is God.

God is *Prema* (love); God expressed *Oṃ*. Therefore, it is the love-expression of God. So, *Oṃ* has come from *Prema*, who is God. Love and its expressions are identical, so *Prema* and *Oṃ* are one and the same.

All the Vedic mantra-s have emerged from *Oṃ*. All the mantra-s have *Oṃ* prefixed. The *Taittirīya Upaniṣad* says, "With *Oṃ*,

Brahmā begins creation." It means the whole creation comes out of sound.

Māṇḍūkya Upaniṣad describes the greatness of this mystical syllable in the following words:

> *Oṃ* is this imperishable word, *Oṃ* is the universe, and this is the exposition of *Oṃ*. The past, present and the future; all that was, is and will be, is *Oṃ*. Likewise, all else that may exist beyond the bounds of time, that, too, is *Oṃ*.
>
> (Verse 1)

The highest conception of *Oṃ* is described in the above verse. The body as we know has come out of the combination of five elements (*pañca-mahābhūta*). In their gross form, they are called ether, air, fire, water and earth. In their subtle form, they are called *Tanmātra*-s or subtle properties from which the gross elements have emerged. They are *śabda* (sound), *sparśa* (touch), *rūpa* (form), *rasa* (taste), and *gandha* (smell). Among the five, the first is sound. Thus it is clear that the world has emerged out of sound.

WHO IS A GURU?

GURU IS ONE who is established in *Brahman* (*Brahma-niṣṭha*). Guru is master. He is the dispeller of ignorance. He is a realized soul. He is simple, humble, serene, still unique. He is ever-united with God. Ego has no place in him. Arrogance has disappeared from him. Lust, rage, greed, infatuation, arrogance and jealousy, the six enemies of man, are totally converted into love, compassion, benevolence, auspiciousness, selfless action, and forgiveness in him. He is the embodiment of all the great virtues. Dualities trouble him not; trials weaken him not. He is formidable in the midst of buffeting waves of happiness and misery in the ocean of rebirth. He is the light that shows the way. He is the door toward *Brahman*. He is the compassionate father and benevolent mother of his disciples. He has attained cosmic consciousness. He knows what is in God's mind and acts accordingly. He follows the path of *dharma*. He has a subtle but powerful influence over the minds and the hearts of people.

People find God in the guru, for there is no ego nor any evil qualities in him. He knows the spirit of the holy scriptures. He lives the spirit of the scriptures. He respects tradition, but gives a new meaning to it. He walks and talks but remains in tune with the Infinite. He is impartial and gives his love to all alike, like the sun which shines over the house of a priest and the hut of a lowborn. He has no passions. He has bid farewell to them. He lives in the highest plane of consciousness. That which the ignorant values has no value for him. He values that which the worldly man despises. Dispassionate as he is, he works for the redemption of the people at large. His heart melts in seeing the misery of others. He lives to serve. His love goes to the animal kingdom, mineral kingdom, and plant kingdom. He sees the same God in everyone and in everything. He hates no one. He preaches and teaches what he practises. He lives and loves for the sake of the divine. Controlled in mind, speech and body, he delights, independent of any object. He is child-like. He speaks of wisdom which vibrates through all the spheres. He is always happy for he is established in Truth. He treats pairs of opposites alike. Heat and cold, pleasure and pain, loss and gain are one and the same to him. He saves people from sin. He guides and protects. He is omnipresent; he is omniscient; he is omnipotent.

Interpretation of the scriptures the guru does spontaneously; the secret of the universe is revealed to him like the fruit that is placed on the cavity of the palm. He exudes the supreme love of God from every pore of his body. He respects masters of the past. He upholds every aspect of dharma. He has no prejudices. He blesses all and tries to make all devotees of God. He is a steadfast seer, separating himself from the body, mind, and intellect. He enjoys the perennial bliss and gives bliss to all who seek.

There is no religion on earth which does not revere a guru. Every religion and its revelation have descended from the mouth of the guru and have developed according to his instructions. God Himself is the first teacher of mankind or *Jagad-guru*. It is the great teachings of the guru that are written in all the great books and religions. Realized as they are, they and their teachings go together, for speech is the essence of man. Who can fathom the glory of such a God-man? Blessed is the land; blessed are the parents who give birth to such a holy personage.

Victory to the guru!

NECESSITY OF A GURU

IN THE THIRTY-FOURTH verse of the fourth chapter of the *Bhagavad-gītā*, the blessed Lord Kṛṣṇa says thus:

> Attain this knowledge by all means; if you prostrate yourself at the feet of the wise, render them all forms of service and question them with a guileless heart, again and again, those wise seers of truth will unfold that wisdom to you.

The necessity of a guru, a man of God-realization, is felt by all seekers after Reality. Even in material matters, the necessity of a teacher is felt. How much more should it be in the case of spirituality, for the path is very subtle. "Who can show the way except the guru?" says Kabir. In the ocean of rebirth, lust and rage are two big rocks through which the boat of life cannot pass unscathed. The thieves of greediness are waiting to steal the spiritual wealth of an individual. There will be sharp showers of arrogance and jealousy and the hurricane of illusion which overturns the ship. The guru alone knows the proper way to escape these dangers and reach the other shore, for he has already reached the other shore and has come, out of compassion, to take others to the other side of the ocean of *saṃsāra*.

Spiritual initiation is a necessary factor in the path of spirituality. During such an initiation, a spiritual power is transmitted from the guru to the disciple. One who receives such transmitted power is a disciple and one who transmits it is a guru. This power is very subtle but powerful. It clears doubts, extinguishes confusion, settles the mind, and the disciple reaches stability and equanimity. He finds his safety in the benign smile of the guru like the young one of the kangaroo finding safety in the pouch of the mother. Now it can stare at one who comes to beat it. Similarly the disciple could stare at death without any fear, for he has reached immortality through the all-encompassing love and protection of the guru. The guru purifies understanding. The *vṛtti*-s, or the deformities of the mind, subside, and mind resides as it were in the higher realms of consciousness. Evil thoughts dare not approach the disciple who is steadfast in his devotion to the guru. He feels the presence of his guru everywhere and at all times. Sant Tukaram says, "Guru makes his disciple one like him. Even though the preparation takes a little time on the part of the disciple, it takes no time for the guru to enter into the disciple to make him one like him." Tukaram says he cannot compare the guru to the touchstone, which only turns the metal into gold. The guru makes his disciple one like him, another touchstone. Groping in darkness, one can never reach the light. Light will come from one who is flooded with it. By the grace of the guru, impossibilities become possibilities and the future possibilities become very near ones. The dull and slow evolution gets compressed and that which has to be attained, after many lives, is at hand to the disciple now. He feels immense joy due to the wide skies of *ānanda* where he can fly with wings of devotion and wisdom. He attains the power to say yes to good thoughts and no to bad ones. He can never be compelled to any sinful deed and is never attracted toward phantasms. Life which was a boredom becomes a life of freedom for he has attained the kingdom of God within. All this was possible due to the grace of the guru who took him slowly to the inner chambers of his heart and showed him the goal of life which is God.

The guru is a veritable treasure house containing rubies of wit and humour and emeralds of truth and divine grandeur. He is deep and sublime but simple and approachable. He is a fire burning the bad karma of his devotees. The guru has the greatness of water to purify and quench the parching thirst of his disciples. He punishes through his silence and teaches through his action. His ways are as mysterious as the ways of God whom he has realized. His grace oozes forth through the pores of his body and shines through his lustrous eyes. "It is impossible to attain *mukti* or emancipation without the grace of the guru", says Purandaradās. A man might be well-versed in the scriptures. He might have renounced the world and might have crucified his flesh, but Truth is revealed only to him who has become the slave of the great master.

GURU AND DISCIPLE

A MANTRA SHOULD be received from a guru. He should be a realized soul. The guru should be pure and sinless. He should practise what he preaches and should have answers for all spiritual problems of humanity. He should know the sacred scriptures and should be compassionate. He should be full of divine love to impart divine wisdom to the qualified disciple or qualify him if he surrenders unconditionally.

The disciple should be inquisitive and pure. It is not enough that he is curious, but he should be serious in the practice of spiritual disciplines. He should please the guru through loving service, reverence, devotion, and dedication. Whenever there has been such a combination of guru and disciple, there has been a wonderful result. Patience and perseverance are the main characteristics of a disciple.

Pleased with the service rendered by the disciple, observing his great qualities, and seeing the right time, the guru should teach the disciple the relationship between God, Soul, and nature. He should guide him, guard him, and lead him to the goal of realization. Surrender on the part of the disciple and protection on the part of the guru are both necessary.

DHYĀNA-YOGA OR YOGA OF MEDITATION

MEDITATION IS deep concentration. The yoga of meditation is the spiritual discipline of concentration on God. Meditation is fathoming the Unfathomable until It reveals Itself. Meditation is focusing the mental and intellectual energy toward one mantra or one thought-power until that mantra reveals its secret. Meditation is the science of realization and the art of communion with God. Meditation is the search after the Supreme Reality in the cavity of our heart. Meditation is the devotional offering of oneself to the Object of Meditation, which is God. Meditation is the struggle of the individual soul to realize and reach the Universal Soul. Meditation is the opening of our being for the direct influx of the Divine Light. Meditation is the discriminative Self-search. Meditation is the headlong plunge into the ocean of cosmic consciousness. Meditation is the door to liberation. Meditation is the highest rung of the spiritual ladder. Meditation leads to knowledge; knowledge leads to love; and love leads to union with God.

MEDITATION IN BHAGAVAD-GĪTĀ

IN THE BHAGAVAD-GĪTĀ Lord Śrī Kṛṣṇa enjoins the following rules for successful meditation:

> In a clean spot on a firm seat with *Kuśa* grass (*darbhāsana*), a deerskin and a cloth spread thereon one below another (*Kuśa* below, deerskin in the middle, and cloth uppermost), neither very high nor very low, one should sit (*Gītā* VI.11).

For meditation, seclusion is a necessary condition, at least for beginners. The practitioner should have been initiated by a competent teacher or guru. He should be by himself (*ekākī*). A clean spot should be selected. The aspirant should have no fear, anxiety, or concern whatsoever regarding the spot where he sits for meditation. In other words, it should be a safe place where he could be free from anxiety and spend as much time as he wants for his practice of meditation. If possible, it is good to have a meditation room in one's home. Of course, to meditate under a tree, on the bank of a river or lake, in a clean cave in the mountains, or even on open ground is very auspicious if those places are clean and calm. To have a meditation room in the house and sit there for meditation is the next alternative for practice. The room should be simple and clean. Any beautiful image of God, symbol, book, or sacred object which inspires and elevates the mind could be kept there. You could light the lamp and burn incense before you begin the practice. You could place fragrant flowers at the feet of the symbol, image or photo of saints or masters. You could also gaze at a candle flame or a flower.

All of the external objects are only symbols of internal love for God and are there to lead one to the rich experience within;

with internal growth, the need for external symbols automatically becomes less. At the same time, it should be kept in mind that through internal growth the external symbols become the living God instead of mere images or symbols. This is fine and wonderful as long as one experiences God internally and externally. If one experiences within, it is spontaneous and natural to experience God without, too. It is a question of the vision with which a man sees things and not the object themselves that matters.

The seat where you sit for meditation should be firm. If it is on the ground, it is well and good for it to be firm. To sever the connection of the mind from the earth vibrations and disturbances, the deerskin was considered to be very auspicious by the yogī-s and Lord Kṛṣṇa supports this view. A seat of *Kuśa* grass (the holy grass used during the sacrifices) was also used by the great *ṛṣi*-s who carried deerskin along with it wherever they went. The seat should not be too high nor too low. The mat of *Kuśa* grass below, the deerskin in the middle, and a cloth uppermost make a good seat. Those who cannot sit on the ground could spread these things over the seat where they sit. Even if they do not have these things, meditation need not be postponed; they could use a tiger skin or only a folded, thick cloth and sit upon that and begin the practice.

When you have arranged the seat, the next question will be how one should sit upon it. Lord Kṛṣṇa says:

> Keeping the trunk, head, and neck straight and steady, remaining firm and looking at the tip of his nose, without looking in other directions. . .(*Gītā* VI.13).

Meditation is the seventh limb or step of the Eight-limbed Yoga or *Rāja*-yoga of Sage Patañjali. After describing the ethical and moral principles to be followed by a practitioner, Patañjali describes the necessity of *āsana* or posture. Even though *Haṭha*-yoga deals elaborately with this subject of various postures, in *Dhyāna*-yoga a posture is stated as a necessary condition. The yogī-s mainly use the lotus posture for meditation.

Sit on the floor; place the right foot on the left thigh and left foot on the right thigh. The two heels should press against the lower part of the abdomen. This is the lotus posture. Keep the trunk, head and neck straight and steady and remain firm. Take a deep breath and be vigilant not to strain yourself. This *āsana* in meditation plays an important part, for it brings steadiness and firmness. *Mudrā*-s, or postures of body, and symbols bring fortitude. Apart from just doing these exercises, we should know the meaning of these postures and gestures which will lead us quickly toward strength of mind, light, and quietude.

The Lotus is the symbol of purity; its blossoming is really the blossoming of consciousness. Therefore, our spiritual centres or *cakras* are compared to lotuses. God, in the *Sahasrāra-cakra*, is Light. The lotus blossoms by the light of the sun, so also our *cakras* blossom by the Divine Light. It has an esoteric meaning, too: just as the lotus remains pure, floating on the water even though its stem is in the mire under the water, similarly, while living in the mire of the world amid waters of *karma*, the mind of a yogī should remain pure and untouched, floating on the water, turning toward the sun of knowledge to blossom into cosmic consciousness or transcendental experiences. The lotus posture brings equilibrium and non-attachment if we practise meditation sitting in that posture.

Siddhāsana is another good posture selected by the *siddha*-s or yogi-s for meditation. Those who cannot practise it or find too much difficulty remaining in *Padmāsana* could sit in *Siddha* posture for meditation. This is very simple but powerful. Sit on the floor, cross your legs; place the right foot on the left thigh. Keep the trunk, head and neck straight. *Āsana* and breathing exercises purify the nerves and eliminate inertia which leads many people into sleep instead of *samādhi* when they sit a long while for meditation. *Āsana* and *prāṇāyāma* drive away this hindrance caused by *tamo-guṇa* and bring steadiness of the mind. *Mukta-padmāsana* and *Baddha-padmāsana* also are very convenient *āsana*-s for meditation. In the former one, just sit cross-legged, placing the right foot on the left thigh and the left on the right thigh; hands are crossed and placed on the thighs. Let the spine be erect and the head straight with the chin on the breast. Now, fix the gaze at the tip of the nose. This is the *Mukta-padmāsana*.

In *Baddha-padmāsana*, remain seated cross-legged just as above, but let the right hand hold the right toe by passing the hand behind the back, then the left hand to the left toe in the same way. Those who cannot do these *āsana*-s, could just sit crosslegged, placing their hands on their thighs and keeping the spine and head erect.

Why should the trunk, head and neck be straight? At the base of the spine lies the serpentine power or *Kuṇḍalinī-śakti* which is dormant and coiled. During meditation, this power rises and, like a serpent, raises its hood, piercing the circles or *cakra*-s which lie along the spinal column. By such awakening, it pierces the veil of ignorance on the one hand and brings various mystical experiences to man on the other. It helps the *Kuṇḍalinī* pass smoothly through the spinal column or *suṣumṇā*.

Apart from this, the *Gītā* advises us to look at the tip of the nose. Why? There are many reasons. Fixing the gaze helps concentration of the mind. If we close our eyes for a long time during meditation and if the mind is not fully aware all that time, then there is the fear of inertia and sleep caused by *tamo-guṇa*. If you keep the eyes open, they see many things and the mind becomes unsteady and wavering, caused by *rajo-guṇa*. Therefore, neither closing the eyes fully nor keeping them wide open, you should keep them half-closed and gaze with both eyes at the tip of your nose. This is *sattva-guṇa*. It causes neither inactivity nor activity, but gives tranquillity leading toward equanimity. Some *yogī*-s practise the other method of fixing their gaze in between the eyebrows. For most people, this may strain the eyes, but fixing the gaze at the tip of the nose should not be too difficult. If your mind is aware, you could close your eyes and fix your mind either in the heart's lotus or in between the eyebrows (*Ājñā-cakra*) or in the thousand-petalled lotus. It is said in *Rāja*-yoga that by concentrating at the tip of your nose, you could gain the power of smelling the most fragrant flowers from any distance. *Haṭha*-yoga says that by gazing at the tip of your nose the muscles of the eyes are strengthened, eyesight improves, and you will get powerful eyes that can calm men of ferocious nature. We should not, however, give much importance to any of these ordinary powers gained through such practices, even though they will follow us unsought when we aim at meditation and realization of the Truth. What next? Lord Kṛṣṇa says:

> And sitting on that seat, concentrating the mind and controlling the functions of the mind and the senses, he should practise yoga for self-purification (*Gītā* VI1: 2).

According to yogī-s, the best time for meditation is *Brahma-muhūrta*, the early hours of the morning between 3.45 and 5.30 A.M.; and when day breaks into night, between 6.30 and 8.00 P.M. Apart from the spiritual significance, the outer nature and the inner nature of man remain calm so that the Great Silence can be felt and meditated upon by the practitioner during those hours. God in His attributeless state is recognized as the Great Silence. One who can meditate on this Great Silence really attains cosmic consciousness, for it silences the ego-consciousness, suspends the dancing wavelets of the lake of mind-stuff (*citta*) and makes man remain as pure being, which is *cit* or consciousness.

Physiologically speaking, man breathes by both nostrils only during the early hours of the morning and early hours of the evening. The rest of the day his breathing is not rhythmic. The one purpose of *Haṭha*-yoga and *prāṇāyāma* is to make breathing rhythmic so that the sun and moon *nāḍī*-s are balanced. If they are balanced, then the breath awakens the hidden universal energy, the *Kuṇḍalinī*, and allows man to take a leap into the Divine. *Ha* is sun; *Ṭha* is moon. *Ha* plus *Ṭha* (yoga) means the path of balancing the sun and moon *nāḍī*-s. These have their exit in the two nostrils, and breathing exercises properly practised purify all the *nāḍī*-s or astral channels through which the spiritual energy moves in the body.

Man breaths with two nostrils during the *sandhi* or periods when day breaks into night and night into day. Therefore, that time has been specified as auspicious for meditation. Of course, when one advances in such practice, one could meditate at any and all times. The suggestion given is especially for the students of *prāṇāyāma*. This is mostly stressed for the students of *Haṭha*-yoga, *Rāja*-yoga, *Kriyā*-yoga, and *Laya*-yoga. The major yoga-s like *Bhakti*, *Jñāna*, and *Karma*-yoga are for advanced yogī-s who never stop at the *siddhī*-s or miraculous powers but who aim at the realization of God and cosmic consciousness.

As soon as one sits for the practice of meditation, one should not suppress thoughts nor impose a mantra on the wandering mind. Instead, the first few minutes can be spent for observation. The intellect should be aware of the turbulent nature of the mind by letting the tenacious mind run wherever it wants. Keep the body in a firm position as described earlier. If the mind runs toward sense objects, then your higher mind should preach to the lower mind thus:

"O Mind, the things that you desire bring utter ruin. The objects to which you cling entangle the soul. For momentary pleasure, everlasting peace should not be forsaken. Happiness for which you run will bring an ocean of miseries; changing objects can never bring changeless joy. The unchangeable abode of peace is God. In Him lies everlasting happiness. So, O Mind, return to your centre."

This method of bringing the mind back to its centre is called *Pratyāhāra* in *Rāja*-yoga and *Vairāgya* (dispassion) in *Bhakti*-yoga. In *Jñāna*-yoga, this is done by discrimination which distinguishes the Real from the unreal.

Once the mind is back to its centre, not from pressure or compulsion but from discrimination and dispassion, then it very easily concentrates on any aspect of God to which it is directed. It is for this purpose that in *Rāja*-yoga, *yama* or restraint, *niyama* or discipline, *āsana* or posture, *prāṇāyāma* or control of life force, and *pratyāhāra* or bringing the mind back to its centre, have been enjoined as the prerequisites for practising meditation. *Yama*, *niyama*, *āsana* and *prāṇāyāma* are the four outer practices, and *pratyāhāra* is the beginning of the inner practice.

Lord Kṛṣṇa uses the term "*Ekāgra-mana*" or singlemindedness. Concentration on mantra or form, on attribute or great silence, or colour, light, or thought or anything brings blessedness. Often the aspirant can see that his mind is easily concentrated when he chooses divine subjects or thoughts which naturally interest his mind. When he imposes alien subjects on his mind or attaches it to some thought without firm faith or devotion, then the mind runs amuck and is never controlled. So, one should begin meditation with some beautiful invocations or prayers. In all the *Upaniṣad*-s, the sages and their disciples used to begin their meditation by some prayer. They would also end their study with meditation and prayer. For example, the *Taittirīya Upaniṣad* begins with this invocation:

> May we propitiate the sun-god; may we propitiate the god of waters; may the god of light be propitious to us; may we propitiate Indra and Bṛhaspati; may Viṣṇu, the God of Preservation, be propitious to us. Salutations to Brahmā; salutations to thee, O wind god; thou art the perceptible God. Of Thee, O visible Reality, will I speak. I will speak of the Truth. May that great Truth protect me; may that Truth protect the speaker; let That guard the speaker. Oṃ, peace, peace, peace.

Such invocations have the immediate wonderful results of bringing the mind to exaltation which, because of the invoked blessings, becomes purified. The purified mind remains steadfast on the thought or object of meditation. It should be remembered here that in the initial stages of the practice of meditation, many bad thoughts, evil thoughts unthought and unsought, may come to the surface. The aspirant should not feel discouraged or disgusted over these nor give up the practice. It is a natural phenomena in meditation that all the evil thoughts, instincts, hallucinations, illusions, delusions, and dark powers hidden in our inner consciousness come to the surface before they die in totality. At this stage, meditation purifies the internal instruments called mind, intellect, ego, and the mind-stuff. It is only after such purification that the seed of mantra can be safely sown in the heart's soil to be watered by repeated meditation until it yields the fruit of spiritual realization or mystical union of soul and God. So, all these processes are essential in this stage called *dhāraṇā* or concentration which is the method of self-purification.

MEDITATION IN UPANIṢAD-S

THE UPANIṢAD-S are the treasure house of ancient wisdom, which have sprung from God as revelations to the *ṛṣi*-s who heard them in their meditation. It will therefore be of great benefit to know about meditation according to the *Upaniṣad*-s. In one of the pithy verses in *Muṇḍakopaniṣad*, the Cosmic Puruṣa or the Universal Form of God, upon which we are asked to meditate, is described thus:

> Fire is the head of Him and His eyes are the sun and moon; the quarters are His organs of hearing and the revealed *Veda*-s are His voice; air is His breath, the universe is His heart, earth lies at His feet. He is the inner Self in all beings. (*Muṇḍaka* II.1.4)

The same types of descriptions are found in the eleventh chapter of the *Bhagavad-gītā* and other *Upaniṣad*-s. This Cosmic Form of God (*Virāṭ-puruṣa*) is to be meditated upon. When we try to think beyond the material universe, when there was no earth, water, fire and air, our highest thinking stops with the idea of ether or a vast space which is the void. This great void from which everything evolves and exists is called *Śūnyatā* in Buddhism. Beyond this void is the kingdom of the spirit, the universal soul, the world soul, the Creator Brahmā, called *Hiraṇyagarbha*. During the cosmic dissolution when the earth enters into water, water is dried by fire, fire is absorbed by air, and air is absorbed into ether, this ethereal void enters into the Creator, Brahmā, who rests in *Parabrahman* or the Supreme Brahman, Who, in the form of Viṣṇu, reposes on the universal energy coiled as the Serpent God on causal waters. The Upaniṣadic verse mentioned above asks us to meditate on that Supreme God in His manifestation. In His unmanifested aspect, He is the Impersonal Spirit and to meditate on the impersonal is difficult.

To meditate on this Cosmic Form is also not easy. But with the mind full of devotion, one has to practise this meditation. Where does one have to meditate?

> The Spirit is this entire universe; He is all the work, austerity and *Brahman* Supreme and Immortal. O fair son, he who knows this, hidden in the secret heart, cuts asunder, even here in this world, the knot of ignorance.
>
> (*Muṇḍaka Upaniṣad* II.1.10)

Solitary meditation is a necessary condition for higher types of meditations. In a calm, serene place one has to practise meditation away from the humdrum of life. It is extremely difficult for the beginner to practise meditation on God in the middle of worldly activities. So, he should go to a retreat and sit and practise to think and concentrate on the higher realities and values of divine life. Then will the inner life open to him; then he has another retreat within which is the cavity of his heart, the seat of God. The eight-petalled lotus, below the heart *cakra* or the *Anāhata-cakra*, is the seat of the Soul (*Haṃsa* or swan) and God dwells in the Soul. Therefore, one has to meditate on the Cosmic Puruṣa in the cavity of the heart in the cardiac centre. The eight petals represent the eight guardian deities (*Dikpālaka*-s): Indra, guardian of the east, Agni of the southeast, Yama of the south, Nirṛti of the southwest, Varuṇa of the west, Vāyu of the northwest, Kubera of the north, and Śiva of the northeast. In the middle is the finite centre of consciousness, the *jīva* or the Individual Soul. The cosmic consciousness is spread within and without from the heart to the thousand-petalled lotus at the top of the brain.

The Individual Soul enveloped by *māyā* (delusion), *karma* (past actions), and *ahaṃkāra* (ego) remains in misery due to the identification with the body, mind, and the intellect, which are the evolvements from *Prakṛti* or kinetic nature. So meditation on the Supreme Reality reveals the Light of Truth which dispels the darkness of ignorance (*Avidyā*) and severs the knots of desire born of such ignorance. Again the *Upaniṣad* declares:

> That which is luminous, That which is smaller than the atoms, That in which are set the worlds and their peoples, That is this; It is *Brahman* immutable; life is That; It is speech and mind. That is this, the true and real; it is That which is immortal; it is into That, that thou must pierce, O fair son, into That, penetrate. (*Muṇḍaka Upaniṣad* II.1.2)

The object of meditation here is the eternal Godhead Itself. It is the luminous Light. It is smaller than the smallest (*Aṇoraṇī-yān*) and greater than the greatest (*Mahatomahīyān*). He is the *Akṣaraṃ Brahma*, i.e. the Indestructible Word. So when we are asked to meditate on the eternal Puruṣa with His Cosmic Form, we are asked to meditate on the eternal Word that is God which is "*Auṃ*".

It is impossible for a weak body and a weak mind to practise such meditation. Of course, a lesser type of meditation makes one strong for higher types. Therefore, to attempt the highest type discussed in the *Upaniṣad* is only for the very strong in all respects. For when the Light descends and nectar flows, the body and the mind should have the power to receive it; if the body and the mind are not strong enough, then various disorders take place. Therefore, it is said elsewhere in the *Upaniṣad-s*: "*Ātman* is not for the weak" (*Nāyam ātmā balahīnena labhyaḥ*).

How could such a type of meditation be understood? The *Muṇḍaka Upaniṣad* discusses that one who meditates is really a strong warrior in life's battle to win a victory over the mind which is tenacious and the senses which are turbulent. If he wins, his is the Kingdom of Heaven, the *Brahma-vihāra*, as the Buddha puts it, and the *Brāhmī-sthitiḥ*, as Lord Kṛṣṇa says in the *Bhagavad-gītā*.

GAYATRIDEVI

PART II

Sandhyā-vandana

MEDITATION ON GĀYATRĪ

Muktā-vidruma-hema-dhavalac-chāyair
mukhais-tryakṣaṇair-
yuktām indu-nibaddha-ratnamukuṭām
tattvārthavarṇātmikām/
Gāyatrīm varadābhayāṅkuśakaśāḥ
śubhram kapālam guṇam
śaṅkham cakram athāravindayugalam
hastair vahantīm bhaje//

I meditate on the (five-faced) Goddess Gāyatrī, whose faces are of the hues of the pearl, coral, gold, blue, black and white (stones), of three eyes (in each face), with jewelled diadems set with the crescent moon, composed of syllables representing the Great Truth, and holding in the (ten) hands, the poses of offering refuge and boons, goad, whip, white skull, rope, conch, discus and two lotuses.

GĀYATRĪ, THE PERSONAL MOTHER

SUPREME, pure consciousness is *Parabrahman*, the impersonal Godhead. This transcendental consciousness as power is Mother. She is known as Gāyatrī. She is the primal cause of everything that was, that is, and that will be. When She manifested the *triguṇa*-s or three qualities, known as *sattva* (poise), *rajas* (passion), and *tamas* (stupor), these three qualities possessing the pure consciousness that is *Parabrahman*, took three forms known as Brahmā, Viṣṇu, and Śiva. Brahmā was possessed by *rajas*, Viṣṇu by *sattva*, and Śiva by *tamas*. Gāyatrī was worshipped by the Trinity as The Mother. When Brahmā, Viṣṇu, and Śiva were just children, Gāyatrīdevī put them into the cradle of Void (*ākāśa*) that was hung by the chains of the four Vedas (wisdom) and with *Oṃ* lullaby, She put them to sleep. Seeing that Her children possessed by *guṇa*-s were sleeping, Devī disappeared.

After a long time, the *Trimurti* got up and began crying. They grew up and were wandering in Void by the power of the *guṇa*-s and then they thought of finding their Mother. They sat in meditation for a long time. As the fire of their austerity was scorching the universe, the Universal Mother, being compassionate, decided to appear before them. Even though She is all-pervasive, still for Her divine *līlā* (sport), She manifested Her divine form.

She was the most beautiful Mother, She wore a red *sāri*. Garlands dangled round Her neck and Her face was like the full moon. She had three eyes and Her forehead carried a round mark of red powder. She had eight arms holding lotuses, mace, conch, and many other shining celestial weapons. She had ankle bells and toerings, bangles and many shining rings, jewels and ornaments, all of which were supraphysical (*aprākṛta*).

She came running for Her children and perspiration was dropping from Her face like pearls. Then, She hurried to Her children and called them by their names as Brahmā, Viṣṇu, and Śiva. The *Trimūrti* ran to their mother, who kissed and caressed them again and again. Holding them in Her arms, She said,

> O divine children, I made you undergo this great agony of separation. I should have come to you long before. I just wanted you to gain powers of creation, preservation, and dissolution through austerity, so that the souls who partake their role in this cosmic *līlā* should see the ideal of austerity and penance shown by you three. I was always with you; yet I was Transcendental. No sooner had you realized Me within yourselves by My grace, than I took a transcendental form also so that the souls hereafter might worship My divine form as the Divine Mother Gāyatrī. I shall be pleased with their worship and confer on them all prosperity and *bhakti*. Now, I am pleased with your devotion. So I shall confer on you the power of creation, preservation, and dissolution. Let Brahmā, by the *rajas* (passion and activity) create; let Viṣṇu, by the quality of *sattva* (equilibrium) maintain and preserve; and let Śiva, by *tamas* (destruction) bring dissolution at the end of cycles. Pray to Me during the times of confusion and difficulty for guidance.

Saying thus, the most blessed Mother disappeared.

This is a mythological description of Devī Gāyatrī. This shows that Gāyatrī is Vedamātā or Mother of the Veda-s, i.e. source of divine wisdom. She is the inseparable power of *Parabrahman*, the Supreme pure consciousness.

Meditation on Gāyatrī Through Breath

While you inhale, you meditate upon Gāyatrī-devī as Sarasvatī with Brahmā in the navel centre.

While holding the breath, meditate upon Her as Lakṣmī with Viṣṇu in the heart centre. She is shining like a blue lotus.

While you exhale, meditate on Gāyatrī as Pārvatī with Śiva in the brow centre. She is shining with purple colour.

They are all part manifestations of Gāyatrīdevī.
May that Supreme Goddess bless you with immortality.

UPANAYANA-SAṀSKĀRA

Upanayana-saṁskāra means the discipline through which the third eye is opened. It is also known as *yajñopavīta-saṁskāra*, or the sacred thread ceremony. This is done to the boy at the tender age of eight by the parents. This is a great initiation given to the boy to maintain celibacy and study the Veda-s or revelations.

The mother is the first guru to child. Under her loving care, he grows and follows her instructions. During the sacred thread ceremony, the mother fixes a loincloth on the boy and teaches:

> My son, treat every woman as your mother up to the age of twenty-four. Until that time, maintain *brahmacarya* or celibacy. Engage your mind in studying the holy scriptures and meditate on the great *Gāyatrī*-mantra which will be imparted to you today. May the Universal Mother Gāyatrī protect you.

This preaching of the mother makes a strong impact upon the mind of the boy. Then the guru blesses him with the sacred thread, chanting the following mantra:

Oṃ Yajñopavītam paramaṃ pavitram
prajāpater yat sahajam purastāt/
āyuṣyam agryam pratimuñca śubhram
yajñopavītam balam astu tejaḥ//

This mantra means,

Oṃ. This holy thread is supremely sacred; progenitors have blessed this thread and by wearing it over the body, one attains longevity. The *yajñopavīta*, or the sacred thread, blesses with strength, radiance and illumination.

The Greatness of the Sacred Thread

Yajñopavīta or sacred thread is given during the ceremony of *Gāyatrī* initiation. That is the symbol of purity. It reminds you of your responsibility to meditate and maintain that purity. It wards off all evil and drives away evil spirits. It is by the initiation of *Gāyatrī*-mantra and the sacred thread ceremony that a boy is treated as a twice-born (*Dvija*), which means that he becomes entitled to study the revelations (Veda-s). The sacred thread is the symbol of transformation of man. It reminds you that you should lead a holy life.

There are three strands in *yajñopavīta* or the sacred thread. The three threads symbolize Brahmā, Viṣṇu and Śiva (Holy Trinity). It also symbolizes many triads such as Mahāsarasvatī, Mahālakṣmī and Mahākālī; the three qualities of nature known as *sattva, rajas* and *tamas*; past, present and future; the three states like wakefulness, dream and deep sleep; the bodies like gross, subtle and causal; the three dimensions known as heaven (*svarga*), earth (*martyaloka*) and nether regions (*pātāla*); the three letters of Oṃ, i.e. A, U and M; the three feet of Gāyatrī, i.e. "*Tat savitur vareṇyaṃ bhargo devasya dhīmahi, Dhiyo yo naḥ pracodayāt*".

The main knot in the thread is known as *Brahmagranthi* or the knot of *Brahmā*. This knot protects our body from disease and evil vibrations.

The most important meaning of the three strands is *iḍā, piṅgalā* and *suṣumṇā nāḍi*-s, through which the *kuṇḍalinī* energy manifests as *prāṇa* and consciousness. As this holy thread is the symbol of sacrifice of ego, it is known as the thread of sacrifice or *yajño-pavīta*.

If somebody dies at home or if a child is born, then, as a purificatory rite, one has to remove the old thread and wear a new one. As a rule, the sacred thread is to be changed once in four months. The householder should always wear two sacred threads. *Brahmacārī*-s should wear only one.

When a new thread is to be worn, the following mantra-s are to be chanted during the act of changing.

Yajñopavītam ity asya mantrasya Parabrahma
ṛṣiḥ, triṣṭup chandaḥ, Paramātmā devatā,
upavīta-dhāraṇe viniyogaḥ/

For the sacred thread, Supreme God is the sage; *Triṣṭup* is the meter; *Paramātmā* or all-pervading consciousness is the presiding deity; such is the affirmation.

Oṃ·Yajñopavītam paramaṁ pavitram
Prajāpater yat sahajam purastāt/
āyuṣvam agryam pratimuñca śubhram
yajñopavītam balam astu tejaḥ//

Oṃ. This sacred (sacrificial) thread is supremely purifying, born, of yore, with Prajāpati (God Brahmā). May this sacred thread endow me with maximum longevity, strength and radiance.

After wearing the new thread, the old one is to be removed. For that, the following mantra is to be chanted while discarding the old sacred thread.

Upavītam bhinnatantum
jīrṇam kaśmaladūṣitam/
visṛjāmi jale brahma-
varco dīrghāyur astu me//

I am discarding in water that sacred thread which has its strands broken and which is decayed and impurified. May the radiance of Brahman and long life be mine.

GĀYATRĪ, THE HIGHEST MEDITATION FOR ILLUMINATION

Gāyatrī meditation is also known as *Sandhyopāsanā* or *Sandhyāvandana*, which means a meditation at dawn and dusk every day. The ancient wisdom of the Himālayas declares that this is the highest meditation for illumination. If one practises this spiritual discipline sincerely, one realizes God in a very short time. So, practise this meditation regularly and attain illumination.

Sandhyā means the meeting period of day and night, i.e. dawn and dusk. *Upāsanā* means meditation. Thus, *Sandhyopāsanā* means the meditation during early morning and early evening. As this meditation is done through the sun which symbolizes the Light of Truth, it is also known as *Sandhyāvandana* or salutations to that Light of Truth.

The early morning and early evening periods are considered as periods of peace or times of spiritual power. The inhalation and exhalation is balanced during those hours and meditation becomes profound and peaceful.

Practice of *Gāyatrī* meditation destroys all *karma*-s and sins. By purifying the heart and the mind, it opens the third eye of illumination. Man lives long with a healthy body, shining like light, and helps humanity in hastening its evolution.

Some practise this meditation four times a day, i.e. early morning, midday, early evening and midnight. Some practise it three times, i.e. dawn, noon, and dusk. When time is a problem, all must practise at least twice a day—that is in the early morning and early in the evening.

"Sins committed consciously or unconsciously during the day

are destroyed by evening meditation and those of the night are reduced to ash by the morning meditation", says Manu. In other words, *Gāyatrī* meditation keeps our mind and heart always pure, and therefore we attain transcendental peace. Sins dare not touch that man who rigidly practises this discipline.

To practise this meditation, the place should be simple, sacred, and secluded. In a secluded spot, the mind remains undisturbed; therefore, concentration becomes easy and spontaneous. In a sacred atmosphere, sacred thoughts alone come. In a simple place, the mind becomes humble. In a place which is frequented by people, where sinful acts are done, and which is luxurious, the mind cannot concentrate and the bad vibration of the place invariably disturbs the meditation. A holy pilgrimage centre, a place where holy men have meditated, the bank of a river, a cave, a mountain retreat, an *āśrama* or hermitage, a confluence where rivers meet, a peaceful garden or the foot of a tree, a house of God or temple, or the shores of an ocean are places conducive to meditation. In one's own house one can sit in one's meditation room, which should be used only for the purposes of prayer, meditation, and worship of God.

When the day breaks into night and night breaks into day, one should practise meditation. Manu, the lawgiver, says, "The *Sandhyā* or *Gāyatrī* meditation that is done before sunrise, while the stars are still visible, is supreme. The meditation begun in the morning when the stars are invisible is medium and the meditation done after sunrise is ordinary."

Similarly, in the evening, the meditation that is done exactly during the sunset is considered as supreme. That meditation is medium that is done after the sunset but before all the stars are visible. If the meditation is done after all the stars are visible, such a meditation is considered as ordinary.

Esoterically speaking, the best time for meditation is when your heart is filled with love for God.

No food is to be taken before the *Gāyatrī* meditation in the morning.

If, due to negligence or some reason, you could not practise your daily meditation, then you have to purify yourself by fasting for a day and a night. As an atonement for negligence, you have to do 1,008 *Gāyatrī-japa* or repetition of *Gāyatrī*-mantra. "If you have given up the *Gāyatrī*-mantra and want to begin that meditation again, then you have to undergo *Upanayanam* or the sacred thread ceremony once again" (Sage Śaunaka).

If one is very ill, the death of someone near and dear has occurred, the house is on fire or the country is in danger, or some calamity has occurred, on such occasions one need not atone for his inability to practise this meditation. Even during such times, to repeat the *Gāyatrī*-mantra mentally averts dangers and brings physical protection and mental solace. At any cost, this daily spiritual discipline must be maintained and should not be neglected with lame excuses. This is the strict word of the sages for our own good. Suppose you are travelling and time is a problem, then meditate on *Gāyatrī* just before you sleep or meditate as soon as you get up in the morning. To repeat whenever you can mentally also brings blessings.

While you chant the mantra if you know the meaning of what you chant, then such a meditation becomes all the more profound and peaceful. Of course, when you chant with faith, the healing vibration of the mantra brings you blessings of peace, whether you know its meaning or not. But knowing the meaning when you meditate, your intellect will have no doubts and therefore the meditation becomes peaceful. Before you begin the meditation, you should chant the name of the sage who has realized this mantra, the prosody of the mantra, and the presiding deity over the mantra. This will have very powerful effects. Similarly, to offer the oblations to the sun-god, to pour the oblations into the fire while chanting the mantra will yield the fruit of such worship very soon. But the highest meditation is prayer for enlightenment and the grace of God. Millions of people would pray for health, wealth, longevity, progeny, etc., and the mantra, even though intended for illumination, also fulfils the desires of its votaries.

When you meditate, sit facing east, west, or north; but while you offer oblations and salutations to the sun-god, you should face the sun-god and do your worship. In other words, the morning meditation should be done facing the east. In the evening, you can face the west and offer your evening oblations. Facing the south is avoided due to the fact described in the scriptures that the abode of the God of Death is in the southern direction.

GĀYATRĪ-SĀDHANĀ

1. One should sit for meditation facing the east in the morning, the north at noon, and the west in the evening.
2. There should be a rosary of *Tulasī*, *Rudrākṣa*, or sandalwood beads.
3. Let the place where you sit for meditation be clean, calm, and sacred.
4. Wash the limbs or bathe before you meditate.
5. Those who meditate on *Gāyatrī* as the Universal Mother may keep a picture of the Divine Mother and worship the Mother before and after the meditation.
6. Those who meditate on *Gāyatrī* as the Light of God can meditate on the sun-god as a symbol of light.
7. Those who meditate on the formless God may meditate on the Light of Truth in the brow centre as a flame of light.
8. As a powerful purificatory rite, you may pour ghee (melted butter) oblations into the fire, chanting "*svāhā*" after repeating the *Gāyatrī*-mantra as follows: "*Oṃ Bhūr Bhuvaḥ Svaḥ, Oṃ Tat savitur vareṇyaṁ, Bhargo devasya dhīmahi, Dhiyo yo naḥ pracodayāt svāhā.*" (After you chant *svāhā*, pour oblations into the fire.)

Gāyatrī for the Fulfilment of Desires

Those who want to pray to Mother Gāyatrī for the fulfilment of any desire may pray for the same before and after the meditation. They may pray for the fulfilment of their desire while they pour ghee oblations into the holy fire. *Gāyatrī*-mantra is chanted mainly for the illumination of the intellect. Yet, there is not the least doubt that it fulfils the desires of the votaries first and then leads to the desireless state.

Men, women, and children who lack memory power can develop the same. They should take a shower and stand in the morning sun, face the east, and chant the *Gāyatrī*-mantra ten times. Within four weeks of this practice, they will develop their memory power and the children will become very intelligent.

Those who want to get a good job and those who always suffer for want of money, and those who want to prosper in their career or business may meditate on the Lakṣmī aspect of Gāyatrī-devī. (Gāyatrī-devī is Sarasvatī, Lakṣmī and Kālī in one.)

1. Do the following *sādhanā* every Friday, regularly. Before you bathe, apply oil mixed with turmeric powder (*haldī*) to your body and then take a bath.
2. Spread a yellow cloth on the seat where you sit for meditation, sprinkle turmeric powder on your sacred thread, wear a yellow cloth, and use yellow flowers to offer to the picture or image of Mother Gāyatrī as Lakṣmī during the *pūjā* or worship. Offer yellow fruits and grains to the Mother and partake the same as *prasāda* after the worship.
3. When you meditate on Gāyatrī as Lakṣmī, visualize the Mother wearing a yellow *sārī*, seated on an elephant.
4. Chant the *Gāyatrī* with "*Śrīṁ*" at the end of the mantra. It is as follows:

Oṃ Bhūr Bhuvaḥ Svaḥ, Oṃ Tat savitur vareṇyaṁ, Bhargo devasya dhīmahi, Dhiyo yo naḥ pracodayāt Śrīṁ. Now have this affirmation: "O Divine Mother, Gāyatrī-Lakṣmī, you are pleased with my devotion. You will bless me with health, wealth, joy, and peace. You will fulfil all my desires. Salutations!"

Do this *sādhanā* every Friday for three months. All impediments will be removed and desires will be fulfilled by the Universal Mother.

Rakṣā-kavaca or Protective Armour

Suppose someone has a seemingly incurable disease or someone is constantly haunted by a demon or possessed by a devil, or someone is always afraid of ghosts and evil spirits. For all such *karmic* and astral troubles, wear the *Rakṣā-kavaca* or the protective armour of Mother Gāyatrī. Usually such talismans are prepared by priests who are adepts in such mantra meditations. But you can do it yourself by following the instructions given below.

On a paper, thin sheet of copper or silver, write five "*Oṃ*" syllables, preferably in *Sanskrit*, as ॐ; one in each of the four corners on the sheet and one in the middle. Now roll it and close one end by folding and put inside the rolled sheet a little sandalwood powder of *kuṁkuma* (the red powder) and chant *Gāyatrī*-mantra ten times. Now it becomes a talisman. Close the other side of the rolled talisman and tie it with a long thread either to the arm or around the neck of the patient. By the power of *Gāyatrī* vibrations, the patient will be healed quickly and all fears will vanish. For retarded children, such a talisman brings healing.

For Having a Child

If a woman's pregnancies constantly end in miscarriage, or if male children alone are born and you have a desire for a baby girl, or girls alone are born and you want a baby boy, for the fulfilment of such a specific desire, the husband and wife should practise the following *Gāyatrī-sādhanā*. Both the husband and the wife should fast on Sundays. You may take some fruit and fruit juice or milk. Taking a shower, you could make a wish for a male or female child and do ten *prāṇāyāma*-s as follows: Inhale deeply through both nostrils and retain the breath and mentally repeat *Gāyatrī*-mantra with three "*yaṁ*" seed-syllables (*bījākṣara*) along with "*Oṃ*" as follows:

> *Oṃ. Yaṁ Yaṁ Yaṁ Bhūr Bhuvaḥ Svaḥ, Oṃ Tat savitur vareṇyaṁ, Bhargo devasya Dhīmahi, dhiyo yo naḥ pracodayāt* and then exhale.

Yaṁ is the seed-syllable of *Varuṇa*, the God of Waters. He is the presiding deity of the genital centre. Therefore, the necessary transformation takes place in the bodies of the husband and the wife.

Now you should hold a rosary of sandalwood beads in your hands and mentally meditate on *Gāyatrī* as a child, wearing white clothes and holding a lotus in Her hand.

After the meditation, you should worship Mother Gāyatrī, offering cooked rice with milk and honey and both of you should partake of that *prasāda* or the sanctified food. It contains the power of *Gāyatrī* that yields the fruit prayed for. In other words, the desired child will be born to that couple in due course. The child that is born will be healthy, beautiful, intelligent, and long-lived.

The following prayer of the Universal Mother Gāyatrī, if chanted with faith and devotion, fulfils all desires of man and leads him to the state of enlightenment.

Namas te devi Gāyatrī Sävitrī tripadākṣare/
ajare amare mātas trāhi mām bhavasāgarāt//

Salutations to you, O Goddess Gāyatrī, the Sun-goddess, of syllables forming three feet (i.e. lines) non-aging and immortal. O Mother, protect me from the ocean of birth and death.

GĀYATRĪ MEDITATION

Gāyatrī meditation is the highest form of meditation known in the Veda-s. By practising this meditation four times a day (early morning, mid-day, evening, and mid-night), one attains perfection of body, mind and spirit.

Gāyatrī is chanted for the attainment of universal consciousness and for the awakening of intuitive powers. The surface meaning of the *Gāyatrī*-mantra is:

> O Existence Absolute, Consciousness Absolute, and Bliss Absolute, Creator of the three dimensions, we meditate on Thy transcendental light. Illumine our intellects.

Gāyatrī meditation destroys all delusions, energizes *prāṇa*, bestows longevity, health, brilliance, and illumination. This mantra is the key to opening the door of cosmic consciousness.

The Practice of Gāyatrī Meditation

1. The best times for the meditation are in the morning just before sunrise and in the evening just before sunset.
2. A clean, secluded place or room should be selected for meditation.
3. A firm seat should be fixed with a deerskin, mat, or cloth.
4. You may sit either in the lotus posture (*Padmāsana*), or the perfect posture (*Siddhāsana* or the *Svastika* posture).
5. You should sit facing east or north.
6. Once you sit in a posture you should not move. As spiritual energy pervades the whole system while chanting the mantra, you should sit firmly. Keep the trunk, head and neck erect.

7. Be fearless. Sit with a firm decision to realize the Truth.
8. Light a camphor or a wick in the room and gaze at it for a few minutes. Close your eyes and visualize the flame in the brow centre through your mind's eye and repeat the *Gāyatrī*-mantra.
9. While you repeat the mantra, meditate on the meaning of the mantra and pray for the vision of Mother Gāyatrī-devī.
10. The *Gāyatrī* is a cosmic rhythm consisting of twenty-four syllables arranged as a triplet of eight syllables each.
11. This is the most sacred Vedic mantra meditated upon during *Sandhyopāsanā.*
12. The Ṛg Vedic *Gāyatrī*-mantra is a prayer for light, for illumination.
13. This mantra is dedicated to God as light and the sun is the symbol of such light.
14. The *Gāyatrī*-mantra is imparted by God Himself to the *ṛṣis* or sages.
15. The *Gāyatrī* is the mother of the Veda-s (the source of Divine Wisdom).
16. This mantra is the key to opening the door of cosmic consciousness.
17. Sage Viśvāmitra is the seer of the *Gāyatrī*-mantra.
18. The *Gāyatrī*-mantra first appears in the *Ṛg Veda* (III.62.10) and later in the *Yajur Veda* and *Sāma Veda* and in the *Upaniṣad*-s. *Gāyatrī* is also called *Sāvitrī*, which is the name of the solar deity. In Reality, it is God as light.
19. This mantra has universality because it is a meditation on light through the sun, which is the same to the whole of humanity.
20. *Gāyatrī* is the power of the Holy Trinity. This mantra confers wisdom, prosperity, purity and liberation.
21. "O Thou Existence Absolute, Consciousness Absolute, and Bliss Absolute, Creator of the three dimensions, we meditate on Thy Transcendental light. Illumine our intellects." This is the surface meaning of the *Gāyatrī*-mantra.
22. *Sandhyopāsanā* or *Gāyatrī-upāsanā* means the meditation which would establish communion with the Supreme Light invoked by the *Gāyatrī*-mantra.

23. *Gāyatrī-upāsanā* is done for attaining Universal Consciousness and awakening the intuitive powers.

Five Techniques of Japa

1. (To memorize the mantra) Utter the mantra loudly and clearly with the correct intonation, pronunciation, and pauses. This is known as *Vaikharī-japa.* Do this thirty-six times.
2. Now mutter the mantra with a very low voice. Lips and tongue alone should move while you pay attention to the meaning of the mantra. This is known as *Upāṁśu-japa.* Do this thirty-six times.
3. Now repeat the mantra mentally. Be absorbed in the central meaning of the mantra. Try to hear the mantra in your heart's *cakra.* This is known as *Madhyamā-japa.* Do this thirty-six times.
4. In the *Maṇipūra-cakra* or the navel centre, you may sometimes see with the inner eye that the mystical words or mantras are written on blossomed petals of the *cakra.* You may see the sound vibrations manifesting through colours. This vision which you get of the sound of the mantra is known as *Paśyantī* or visible sound.
5. Now, just enter into perfect silence. In the beginning, mentally meditate on "*Oṃ*". Then merge in Transcendental Peace or Silence of thy *Ātman.* This is known as *Parā.*

Practice the *Gāyatrī*-mantra at least ten times every morning and ten times in the evening. One who repeats the mantra 108 times in each sitting will attain radiance soon. One who repeats the mantra 1008 times with sincerity and devotion in each sitting will attain illumination in forty days.

While you repeat the mantra, meditate on the meaning of the mantra and pray for the *darśana* of Mother Gāyatrī-devī.

Gāyatrī meditation destroys all delusions, energizes *prāṇa,* bestows longevity, health, brilliance and illumination.

Arrange a firm seat in a quiet place or room. Light a camphor or a wick and gaze at it for a few minutes. Now close your eyes and visualize the flame in the brow centre through your mind's eye and repeat the *Gāyatrī*-mantra.

Blessings of Gāyatrī-mantra

Unless the intellect is illumined, the Truth remains unrevealed. Intellect veiled by *tamas* (dark forces) and *rajas* (passion), however clever and sharp it might be in worldly matters, is not going to bring peace and true happiness. Intellect purified by *sattva-guṇa* or tranquillity attains the state of illumination. The light of *Gāyatrī*-mantra, removing the rust and dust of stupor and passions of the mind's mirror, reflects the Truth in it by which the mind is illumined. Man attains a transcendental peace by such illumination and all actions he does after that experience will uplift the entire society. He becomes a blessing to humanity.

The *prāṇa* energy that was wasted day after day due to *tāmasika* and *rājasika* activities now takes an upward turn and the holy *Gāyatrī*-mantra protects the *prāṇic* energy and blesses man with health, radiance, courage, and inexhaustible strength.

Gāyatrī light blesses with the power of celibacy, power of truthful, sweet speech, power of healing, and power of transmitting the spiritual energy into others.

Good health, longevity, non-possessiveness, humility, spiritual insight, selfless service, sacrifice, understanding, forbearance, universal friendship, unflinching devotion to Truth, cosmic consciousness, and cosmic love and other divine virtues manifest in man by the practice of *Gāyatrī*-mantra.

Man commits errors and sins due to the darkness of ignorance. *Gāyatrī* blesses with the Light of Truth so that man cannot fall into the clutches of karma and rebirth. By opening our third eye of wisdom, it reveals the past, present and future to us and leads us gently toward the Kingdom of Heaven. Transforming our energy into divine love and creativity, the light of *Gāyatrī* makes our whole life a life divine.

Gāyatrī-mantra removes all fears. It is the best cure for all ills. It destroys *karma* and blesses with liberation. Wherever *Gāyatrī*-mantra is chanted, devils and evil spirits are driven away by the fire of that Word of God.

GĀYATRĪ AND PURUṢA-SŪKTA
(The description of God as Cosmic Person)

Gāyatrī-mantra has been accepted by all the sages of the Himalayas as the greatest mantra. In India, especially among orthodox Hindus, it is never chanted publicly, for it is the most sacred mantra. The *Gāyatrī* is imparted to the son by the father at the time of the investiture of the sacred thread ceremony (*Upanayanaṁ*). All the great masters of Vedic religion invariably repeat this mantra. The main reason for such secrecy is that people who lack discrimination, who do not practise spiritual discipline, misuse such mantras, which are meant for spiritual illumination. This *Gāyatrī*-mantra contains the power of God. Imparted by the father to his son or from the guru to the disciple, traditionally this was kept secret because it was the most sacred mantra. And presently, even though many may read this mantra from books, it works and reveals God by the observance of yogic diet, spiritual discipline, and yoga practice. This mantra, if given in an initiation by the guru and practised regularly by the disciple, bestows all blessedness, power, brilliance, and illumination. The short version of the *Gāyatrī* text reads thus:

Oṃ Bhūr Bhuvaḥ Svaḥ
Oṃ Tat Savitur Vareṇyam/
Bhargo Devasya Dhīmahi
Dhiyo Yo Naḥ Pracodayāt//

The idea intended is:
O effulgent light that has given birth to all the *loka*-s or spheres of consciousness, O God who appears through the shining sun, illumine our intellect.

This is the surface meaning of the text. This mantra contains all the important *bīja*-mantras.

In this short version of *Gāyatrī*-mantra, *Oṃ* symbolizes God, *Bhūḥ* represents earth, *Bhuvaḥ* represents the atmospheric regions covering all the subdivisions of semigods and demigods up to the sun. *Svaḥ* represents the third dimension or celestial region, known as *Svarga-loka* and all the luminous *loka*-s above.

The Veda-s contain the wisdom of God. The essence of the Veda-s is in the *Pusuṣa-sūkta* or the meditation on Cosmic Person that is God, and the essence of *Puruṣa-sūkta* is in these *vyāhṛti*-s. Thus, *Bhuḥ* is *Ṛg Veda*, *Bhuvaḥ* is *Yajur Veda*, and *Svaḥ* is *Sāma Veda*. The fifteen mantra-s in the *Puruṣa-sūkta* explain in detail these three rhythms of *Gāyatrī*. Thus, *Bhūḥ* is explained in the first five mantra-s, *Bhuvaḥ* in the second five and *Svaḥ* in the last five mantra-s of the great prayer of *Puruṣa-sūkta*. All this is explained in the following pages.

These are the five stanzas explaining the inner meaning of the rhythm *Bhūḥ*:

I

Oṃ. Sahasraśirṣā puruṣaḥ
Sahasrākṣaḥ sahasrapāt/
Sa bhūmim viśvato vṛtvā
Atyatiṣṭhad daśāṅgulam//

Oṃ. The Primal Person has a thousand heads, thousand eyes, thousand feet. Pervading the entire universe, He transcends everything. (Is ten finger widths above, which means transcendental. Here the number thousand means infinite.)

II

Oṃ. Puruṣa evedam sarvam
Yad bhūtam yac ca bhavyam/
Utāmṛtatvasyeśānaḥ
Yad annenātirohati//

Oṃ. All this is that Supreme Person—that which was, that

which will be. He is the Lord of immortality. When embodied, He shows as if He grows by the food (whereas He is the essence).

III

Oṃ. Etāvān asya mahimā
Ato jyāyāṃśca pūruṣaḥ/
Pādo 'sya viśvā bhūtāni
Tripād asy'mṛtam divi//

The glory of this Primeval Person is manifested in this universe which is His creation. He is infinitely greater than this universe. This whole universe with all animate and inanimate objects is only one-quarter of this Supreme Person. Three-fourths of His power and manifestation is shining above in the transcendental spheres which are indestructible.

IV

Oṃ. Tripād ūrdhva udait puruṣaḥ
Pādo 'syehābhavat punaḥ/
Tato viṣvaṅ vyakrāmat
Sāśanānaśane abhi//

The invisible three-fourths effulgence of this Cosmic Reality is established in spheres of light. Only His one-fourth effulgence appears here. Then This [manifested one-fourth power, this Primal Person] is pervading all (those who manifest hunger and thirst), and all the inert matter, too [with various names and forms.]

V

Oṃ. Tasmād virāḍ ajāyata
Virājo adhi pūruṣaḥ/
Sa jāto atyaricyata
Paścād bhūmim atho puraḥ//

The universe of varied forms emerged from this Primal Person. Holding this cosmos [as His body,] the Supreme Being manifested. He created the celestials, animals and human beings and the earth by His own power, even though He was always transcendental.

These are the five stanzas explaining the inner meaning of the rhythm *Bhuvaḥ*:

VI

Oṃ. Yat puruṣeṇa haviṣā
Devā yajñam atanvata/
Vasanto asyāsīd ājyam
Grīṣma idhmaḥ śaradd haviḥ//

Later, [to propitiate this Cosmic Truth,] the celestials made a [symbolic mental] fire-sacrifice. To this fire-sacrifice, spring became the oblation, summer became the fire-wood, the autumn became the main offering.

VII

Oṃ. Saptāsyāsan paridhayaḥ
Trisapta samidhaḥ kṛtāḥ/
Devā yad yajñam tanvānā
Abadhnan puruṣam paśum//

For this [sacrifice], seven [meters] are the boundaries. Twenty-one [principles] are the fire-sticks. To this sacrificial pillar, gods bound the Cosmic Truth Itself [by the cord of mantra for their realization.]

VIII

Oṃ. Tam yajñam barhiṣi praukṣan
Puruṣam jātam agrataḥ/
Tena devā ayajanta
Sādhyā ṛṣayaś ca ye//

They installed the Cosmic Person over the holy grass and

invoked Him there, the One who was before [the creation and the object of the great fire-sacrifice]. Thus, the celestials and the perfected beings [joining together] performed the [mental] fire-sacrifice, [the great meditation, keeping Him as the main oblation].

IX

Oṃ. Tasmād yajñāt sarvahutaḥ
Sambhṛtam pṛṣadājyam/
Paśūṃs tāṃścakre vāyavyān
Āraṇyān grāmyāṃś ca ye//

There emerged a curd that contained the ghee (clarified butter) from the altar of the fire-sacrifice in which the Cosmic Being Himself was the highest oblation. Later, birds that fly, animals of the forest, and the animals that move in villages were created.

X

Oṃ. Tasmād yajñād sarvahutaḥ
ṛcaḥ sāmāni jajñire/
Chandāṁsi jajñire tasmād
Yajus tasmād ajāyata//

All [*mantra*-s, known as] *Rik*, *Yajus*, *Sāman*, and the metres emerged out of that [in which the Self of all selves was the main oblation].

These are the five stanzas explaining the inner meaning of the rhythm *Svāhā*:

XI

Oṃ. Tasmād aśvā ajāyanta
ye ke cobhayād ataḥ/
Gāvo ha jajñire tasmāt
Tasmāj jātā ajāvayaḥ//

Horses, animals having two-lined teeth, cows, goats, sheep, and the like were born of this Cosmic Sacrifice.

XII

Oṃ. Yat puruṣaṃ vyadadhuḥ
Katidhā vyakalpayan/
Mukham kim asya kau bāhū
kā ūrū pādā ucyete//

Into how many parts did they divide this Cosmic Being when they decided to pour Him as the oblation? Which is His face? Which are His arms? His thighs and feet?

XIII

Oṃ. Brāhmaṇo 'sya mukham āsīt
Bāhū rājanyaḥ kṛtaḥ/
ūrū tad asya yad vaiśyaḥ
Padbhyām sūdro ajāyata//

Brahmin-s (priests) emerged from the mouth, *Kṣatriya*-s (warriors) from the arms, *Vaiśya*-s (tradesmen) from the thighs, *Śūdra*-s (men of service) from the feet of this Cosmic Person.

XIV

Oṃ. Candramā manaso jātaś
Cakṣos sūryo ajāyata/
Mukhād indraś cāgniś ca
Prāṇād vāyur ajāyata//

From His mind emerged the moon, sun from His eyes, Indra (Lord of the first heaven) and Agni (fire-god) from His mouth, and the Cosmic Breath (Vāyu, the air) emerged from His breath (*prāṇa*).

XV

Oṃ. Nābhyā āsīd antarikṣam
Śīrṣṇo dyauḥ samavartata/
Padbhyām bhūmir diśaḥ śrotrāt
Tathā lokān akalpayan//

Atmosphere emerged out of His navel, sphere of light (*Dyuloka*) from His head, earth from His feet, directions from His ears. Thus, the celestials (*deva*-s) created all spheres (*loka*-s) from His Cosmic Body.

Oṃ. Yajñena yajñam ayajanta devās
Tāni dharmāṇi prathamāny āsan/
Te ha nākam mahimānaḥ sacanta
Yatra pūrve sādhyāḥ santi devāḥ//

Thus, the gods worshipped (the God of gods mentally) through sacrifice. The technique used in that *yajña* became the first law of life. The meditation on this Cosmic Form of God leads the devotees to the highest heaven where the masters and angels dwell.

Oṃ. Śāntiḥ, Śāntiḥ, Śāntiḥ

VIŚVĀMITRA

VIŚVĀMITRA was a king of India. Once he went hunting in a Himalayan forest. He and his troop felt hungry and fatigued after the hunt. They saw a hermitage and discovered that it was the hermitage of Brahmarṣi Vasiṣṭha (a *Brahmarṣi* is a sage of cosmic consciousness). The king approached the sage and saluted him. Sage Vasiṣṭha welcomed him and offered him a seat. When the king told the sage that he and his retinue were very much in need of food and rest, the sage immediately called Kāmadhenu, the cow of plenty, and requested her to feed all the people and the king. The wish-cow produced the food by a mere act of will and fed all of them. They were amazed at the wish-fulfilling power of the cow (symbolizing infinite yogic powers).

King Viśvāmitra approached Sage Vasiṣṭha and said, "O Venerable Sage, I am pleased with your wish-cow. Why should you have such a cow which is capable of feeding millions by mere wish? There are only a few of you living in this hermitage, whereas I, the king, have to feed millions every day in my palace. This wish-cow will be very useful to me. I shall give you thousands of cows in exchange for this cow. I need it; please allow me to take this cow of plenty with me."

Sage Vasiṣṭha said, "O King, this cow is a very special cow sent by God from the plane of Truth. Only those who have realized *Brahman*, or Truth, are given this cow of plenty. Even if you offered your whole kingdom in exchange for this cow, I would not part with her."

King Viśvāmitra flew into a rage. He said, "O Sage, do not forget that I am the king. You have insulted me by refusing my request. Now I have to take the cow by force."

"Try if you can", said the sage. The king ordered his men to take the cow by force. As soon as they tried, the cow, at the behest of Sage Vasiṣṭha, produced thousands of celestial men holding celestial weapons, and the king's troops were driven out. Stung by hatred and anger, King Viśvāmitra fought with Sage Vasiṣṭha. Chanting powerful mantra-s, Brahmarṣi Vasiṣṭha held his *brahma-daṇḍa*, or monk's staff, and challenged the king. All the arrows which King Viśvāmitra discharged at Sage Vasiṣṭha were devoured by the monk's staff. The king exhausted all his weapons, and the miraculous staff then came to strike at the king. Finally, the king realized the power of a *Brahmarṣi*. He prayed for forgiveness. Sage Vasiṣṭha, being kind and compassionate, forgave him and withdrew his staff, the *brahma-daṇḍa*.

King Viśvāmitra still felt insulted. He thought that all his position and possessions, power and wealth, rulership and kingdom, health and beauty were nothing compared to the *brahma-tejas* (effulgence) of Sage Vasiṣṭha. He ran away and sat under a tree where he wept like a child. "Oh!" he cried, "all these days I thought that power and position were everything. Now I realize that nothing is greater than the knowledge of Truth. Endless universes are at the command of that Sage Vasiṣṭha. The cow of plenty and the miraculous staff are just symbols of his immense spiritual powers. Ah! How shall I reach that *Brahmarṣi* status? How shall I acquire all those miraculous powers? How shall I know the secret of initiation? All these years of my life have been wasted. I shall never go back to my palace. I shall renounce my queen, sons and kingdom, and go to a forest in the Himalayas to practise meditation. I must acquire all those powers which Sage Vasiṣṭha has and I must retaliate; I must challenge his powers. Oh, I must!"

Look at the power of *māyā*! The thought of retaliation remained with the king even while he took the decision to meditate on the Truth!

Renouncing his kingdom, family and children, Viśvāmitra entered into a formidable forest of the Himalayas. Accustomed to the royal palace, timely food, and rest, Viśvāmitra felt restless, fatigued, and miserable. He was all alone without any attendants or servants and did not know what he should do. He knew very little about *yoga*, *prāṇāyāma* and meditation, but his ego prevented him from asking the guidance of Sage Vasiṣṭha. *I must, I will*, he thought, and that powerful urge sustained him.

Viśvāmitra climbed a huge peak of the Himalayas and bathed in the streams of the holy Ganges River. Then he sat on a rock and looked around. It was so calm and quiet there. An ideal place for meditation! The sky-kissing peaks of the Himalayas! The abode of sages, angels, and Lord Śiva! Holy Ganges springing from the matted locks of Śiva! The charming smile of Lord Śiva in his austere meditation! *I should practise austerity and meditate like Lord Śiva on the Cosmic Self*, thought Viśvāmitra.

Practising *prāṇāyāma* (rhythmic breathing), Viśvāmitra meditated on the Cosmic Self. By practising self-analysis, he separated his mind from the body and developed the power of detachment. Then he conquered the mind through right discrimination and stilled all his thoughts. Yogic fire and smoke emerged from the crown of his head and began burning the higher spheres. Indra, the head of the celestials, was frightened, thinking that Viśvāmitra might attempt to occupy his throne by his powers. To spoil his *tapasyā* (austerity), Indra sent a beautiful celestial nymph named Menakā who sang and danced before Viśvāmitra. She disturbed his meditation and attracted his heart with her bewitching smile.

Viśvāmitra fell victim to *rajas* (passion) and lived happily with Menakā for a year in the forest. A female child, whom they named Śakuntalā, was born to them. At length, Viśvāmitra realized the power of *māyā* and went to another forest in the Himalayas. He renounced Menakā and her child. Menakā, the celestial nymph who had come to destroy his austere penance, left the baby girl in that forest and returned to her celestial abode. A sage named Kaṇva, who was wandering in that forest, heard the cry of the baby Śakuntalā. He rescued her and took her to his hermitage where he brought her up.

Renouncing food and drink, Viśvāmitra took a bold decision to attain the highest spiritual powers. He stood on one leg with uplifted arms and meditated on *Brahman* for a number of years. The three worlds were reached by the yogic fire of his austerity. Indra sent another celestial nymph named Rambhā to spoil the penance of Viśvāmitra. Rambhā tried to entice him with her charm and enchant him with melodious music. Viśvāmitra's meditation was shaken and he opened his eyes. Being aware of his past folly, he decided not to yield to the desire of flesh. He became very angry at Rambhā, as he knew she had come to spoil his *tapasyā*. Angrily, he uttered a curse which turned her into a rock. Immediately Viśvāmitra saw that his powers gained through austerity were spoiled by a moment's anger. The first time lust, and now anger had spoiled his penance, and he realized that the spiritual path is as hazardous as walking on a razor's edge.

But Viśvāmitra's spirit was indefatigable. He climbed another peak of the Himalayas. Motionless and holding his breath for a number of years, he acquired great spiritual powers.

During that time, India was ruled by King Triśaṅku. He wanted to perform a great fire-sacrifice which would send him to the celestial region (*svarga*) in his human body. He approached Sage Vasiṣṭha, his family guru, to perform the fire-sacrifice. Sage Vasiṣṭha refused to perform the sacrifice, saying that it was against divine law for a human being to go to heaven in his earthly body. The king was angry at this rejection and approached Viśvāmitra, Vasiṣṭha's opponent.

Viśvāmitra, who wanted retaliation, took this as a wonderful opportunity to display his yogic powers. He returned with the king to the palace and organized the great fire-sacrifice. Becoming the head priest himself, Viśvāmitra performed the fire-sacrifice successfully and, by his yogic power, sent King Triśaṅku to the celestial region of Indra.

Indra and the celestials saw the king entering heaven with his earthly body and they pushed him back to earth. While King Triśaṅku was falling from heaven, his head below and legs up, he cried with agony and prayed, "Viśvāmitra, Viśvāmitra, protect me." Sage Viśvāmitra saw the king falling from heaven and, with his yogic power, stopped the fall. He said to the king, "O King Triśaṅku, stop; stop there. You need not worry. I shall create a new heaven for you where you are and shall vanquish the pride of Indra and the celestials." So saying, Sage Viśvāmitra created a new stellar system and a heaven for Triśaṅku. Even today, Triśaṅku shines as a star in the sky!

Again Viśvāmitra lost all his yogic powers by using them for ulterior gains. He felt despondent because he had not achieved his highest goal. He again took a firm decision not to move from his meditation until he attained illumination. His spirit was invincible!

He selected the highest peak of the Himalayas. Withdrawing his mind from the senses, he meditated on the eternal *Brahman*. Seasons rotated; years passed, but Viśvāmitra sat motionless, his gaze fixed between the eyebrows. So great was his penance this time that the yogic fire which emerged from the crown of his head reached *Satyaloka*, the abode of Creator Brahmā. To save the world from the scorch of Viśvāmitra's yogic fire, Brahmā appeared to him and blessed him, "O my son, I am pleased with your penance. You have attained the highest. You are a great sage (*Maharṣi*) now. You will be a *Brahmarṣi* when you are blessed by Sage Vasiṣṭha." Saying these words, Brahmā disappeared.

Sage Viśvāmitra was frustrated. "Again I have to go to Vasiṣṭha for his blessings to become a *Brahmarṣi*! Oh, no! I cannot do that. So long as Vasiṣṭha lives, I cannot become a *Brahmarṣi*. Perhaps if I kill him, then I can be a *Brahmarṣi*!" Thinking thus, Viśvāmitra went to the hermitage of Brahmarṣi Vasiṣṭha at midnight. Carrying a huge rock to hurl on Vasiṣṭha's head, he stood near the gates of Vasiṣṭha's hermitage and waited for him to pass by that way to the river for his morning meditations!

Viśvāmitra heard Brahmarṣi Vasiṣṭha speaking to his wife, Arundhatī. "Arundhatī", Vasiṣṭha said, "Viśvāmitra is such a great man that he is very near to the attainment of the status of *Brahmarṣi*, but..."

Arundhatī said, "But what? Will you not bless him with that status if he is worthy of it?"

"Of course I will", said Vasiṣṭha, "provided he comes to me."

Viśvāmitra, who was listening to this conversation, felt ashamed of his hatred toward such a divine sage. He threw the rock away and rushed to Brahmarṣi Vasiṣṭha and fell prostrate at his feet.

"Now you have become a *Brahmarṣi*", said Vasiṣṭha to Viśvāmitra. "You have shown to the world that the human spirit is invincible and accepts no defeat. You conquered lust, anger, greediness, attachment and arrogance one by one through your austerities and meditations. The last barrier was jealousy. Now you have conquered that enemy also. Hail Brahmarṣi Viśvāmitra!"

As Vasiṣṭha touched the brow centre of Viśvāmitra, his third eye opened and he saw the seven rhythms with which the cosmos was created. The sacred *Gāyatrī*-mantra with its seven *vpāhṛti*-s or rhythms was revealed to him at that time, thus:

> Oṃ Bhūḥ, Oṃ Bhuvaḥ Oṃ Svaḥ Oṃ Mahaḥ
> Oṃ Janaḥ Oṃ Tapaḥ, Oṃ Satyaṁ,
> Oṃ Tat Savitur Vareṇyam,
> Bhargo Devasya Dhīmahi
> Dhiyo Yo Naḥ Pracodayāt//
> Oṃ Āpo Jyotiḥ
> Raso-Mritaṃ Brahma
> Bhūr Bhuvaḥ Svar-Oṁ

Brahmarṣi Viśvāmitra experienced cosmic consciousness. He was established in that highest consciousness forever and became immortal!

Man may fall many times in his spiritual journey, but let him never give up until he attains the Supreme!

JAYA BRAHMARṢI VIŚVĀMITRA!

PRACTICE OF SANDHYĀ-VANDANA

Sandhyā-vandana is the greatest discipline of 16 *kriyās* in which the universal light of *Gāyatrī* is invoked. Practice of this meditation leads to cosmic consciousness. This is to be practised during the early hours of the morning and evening. Those who want to practise it intensely can meditate four times a day, that is, early morning, mid-day, early evening, and midnight. Those who observe this *sādhanā* or discipline rigidly before the sunrise and soon after the sunset, which are considered as the hours of power, shall certainly have their third eye of wisdom opened within a short period of time. Those who cannot meditate four times a day should at least observe twice, that is in the morning and in the evening.

In the whole of *Sandhyā-vandana*, there are sixteen *kriyā*-s: twelve are to be observed before the great meditation and the thirteenth *kriyā* is the great meditation on *Gāyatrī*. After the meditation, the remaining three are to be observed.

These sixteen *kriyā*-s or esoteric, mystical disciplines, are:

1. *Ācamana*
2. *Prāṇāyāma*
3. *Saṅkalpa*
4. *Mārjana*
5. *Apa prāśana*
6. *Aghamarṣaṇa*
7. *Arghya-pradāna*
8. *Bhū-śuddhi*
9. *Bhūta-śuddhi*
10. *Āsana-vidhi*
11. *Gāyatrī-hṛdaya-pārāyaṇa*

12. *Gāyatrī-nyāsa*
13. *Gāyatrī-dhyāna*
14. *Tarpaṇa*
15. *Upasthāna*
16. *Gāyatrī-prasthāpana*

These sixteen *kriyās* are to be studied under the guidance of a spiritual teacher trained in this technique.

Even before you begin the very first *kriyā* known as *Ācamana*, there are certain prayers to be offered as soon as you get up in the morning until you bathe and get ready for meditation. The whole detail of this, along with the prayer mantra-s as they are observed since time immemorial in the Himalayan tradition, will be narrated in these pages.

Begin the Day with Prayer

Chant as you get up from bed in the early morning:

Uttiṣṭhottiṣṭha Govinda
Uttiṣṭha garuḍadhvaja/
Uttiṣṭha kamalākānta
Trailokyam maṅgalam kuru//

Awake and arise (in my heart), my Lord, Govinda, (as divine consciousness). Awake, my God, who flies on the eagle. Arise, O spouse of Goddess of Prosperity. Bless all three worlds with peace.

This prayer brings very high vibrations of expansion of consciousness to soar high in your activities and attain prosperity and peace.

Then look at both of your palms, holding them together, and pray:

Karāgre vasate Lakṣmī
Karamadhye Sarasvatī/
Karamūle tu Govindaḥ
Prabhāte karadarśanam//

(I meditate on) Lakṣmī, the Goddess of Prosperity, residing at the tip of the fingers; and Sarasvatī, the Goddess of Wisdom, in the mid-palm; and on Govinda, the Lord of the Universe, at the base of the palm. (I meditate on God's powers) early in the morning, seeing (Him in) my palms.

Samudravasane devi
    Parvatastanamaṇḍite/
Viṣṇupatni namas tubhyam/
    Pādasparaśam kṣamasva me//

O Mother Earth, spouse of Lord Viṣṇu, whose robes are the oceans, bosom the mountains, forgive me (your child) who am just to walk over you.

Now you should bathe or, if it is inconvenient for any reason, wash your face and limbs. As you bathe or wash, chant the following mantra or mentally repeat it:

Gaṅge ca Yamune caiva
    Godāvari Sarasvati/
Narmade Sindhu Kāveri
    Jale 'smin sannidhim kuru//
Puṣkarādyānī tīrthāni
    Gaṅgādyāḥ saritas tathā/
Āgacchantu pavitrāṇi
    Snānakāle sadā mama//

Bless with thy presence, O holy rivers Ganges, Yamunā, Godāvarī, Sarasvatī, Narmadā, Sindhu and Kāverī. May Puṣkara, and all the holy waters and the rivers such as the Ganges, always come at the time of my bath.

After bathing, put on the meditation clothes, chanting *Oṃ Namo Nārāyaṇāya* (*Oṃ*. Salutations to Lord Nārāyaṇa, the Heavenly Father) twelve times.

If the sun is not visible due to clouds or you cannot go out due to weather conditions or for any other reason, then you meditate on the sun in your brow centre, chanting the following mantra:

Dhyeyaḥ sadā savitṛmaṇḍala-madhyavartī
Nārāyaṇaḥ sarasijāsanasanniviṣṭaḥ/
Keyūravān makarakuṇḍalavān kirīṭī
Hārī hiraṇmayavapur dhṛtaśaṅkhacakraḥ//

The Supreme Lord, Nārāyaṇa, who resides in the Solar orb, seated on the lotus seat, wearing armlets, alligator-shaped ear-rings, and diadem, garlanded, having a golden body (and) holding the conch and the discus, should always be meditated upon.

Now do the sun-salutation. Those who know the sun-salutation posture or yoga with its twelve limbs can do the sun-salutation by using one mantra for each limb. Those who do not know that posture or cannot do it due to any reason can meditate on the sun-god by joining their palms and chanting the following mantra-s.

Begin your meditation with the sun-salutation. In the beginning, sit erect, join the palms, close your eyes, and meditate on the pillar of light up and down the spine and in the middle of the brows. Chant these twelve mantra-s which are the twelve names of the solar deity, as follows:

1. Oṃ Mitrāya namaḥ
   Salutations to Mitra, the bestower of universal friendship.
2. Oṃ. Ravaye namaḥ
   Salutations to Ravi, the bestower of radiance.
3. Oṃ Sūryāya namaḥ
   Salutations to Sūrya, the dispeller of darkness.
4. Oṃ Bhānave namaḥ
   Salutations to Bhānu, the shining principle.
5. Oṃ. Khagāya namaḥ
   Salutations to Khaga, the all-pervading.

6. Oṃ. Pūṣṇe namaḥ
   Salutations to Pūṣan, the mystic fire.
7. Oṃ. Hiraṇyagarbhāya namaḥ
   Salutations to Hiraṇyagarbha, the golden-coloured one [who brings healing].
8. Oṃ Marīcaye namaḥ
   Salutations to Marīci, the light.
9. Oṃ Ādityāya namaḥ
   Salutations to Āditya [one aspect of Viṣṇu].
10. Oṃ Savitre namaḥ
    Salutations to Savitā, impeller.
11. Oṃ Arkāya namaḥ
    Salutations to Arka, the remover of afflictions.
12. Oṃ Bhāskarāya namaḥ
    Salutations to Bhāskara, the cosmic brilliance.

Oṃ. Śrī-Savitre Sūryanārāyaṇāya namaḥ.
Mitra-Ravi-Sūrya-Bhānu-Khaga-Pūṣā-
Hiraṇyagarbha-Marīcyāditya-Savitrarka-
Bhāskarebhyo namo namaḥ.

Oṃ. Salutations (to the effulgent power of) Lord Nārāyaṇa manifesting through the sun-god. Again and again salutations to (the twelve aspects of light of God, known as) Mitra, Ravi, Sūrya, Bhānu, Khaga, Pūṣā, Hiraṇyagarbha, Marīci, Āditya, Savitṛ, Arka, Bhāskara.

Keep a cup of pure water. Hold a spoon in the left hand and take a spoonful of water from the cup and pour it onto the right palm, holding the hand like a conch and chant the following mantra:

Akālamṛtyuharaṇam sarvavyādhivināśanam/
Sūryapādodakaṃ tīrthaṃ jaṭhare dhārayāmy aham//

I hold in my stomach the holy water which has washed the feet of God Sun—the holy water which wards off untimely death and destroys all diseases.

Sit facing east or north and then chant the purificatory mantra:

Oṃ. Apavitraḥ pavitro vā sarvāvasthāṃ gato 'pi vā/
Yaḥ smaret Puṇḍarīkākṣaṃ sa bāhyābhyantaraḥ
śuciḥ//

Oṃ! Whether impure or pure, under all conditions he who thinks of the Lotus-eyed One, [becomes] pure internally and externally. (Saying thus, sprinkle the water over the head.)

Ācamana

Ācamana or three times sipping the holy water is for purifying the body, mind, and the soul. It purifies the gross, astral, and causal bodies as well. This discipline calms our senses, stops the oscillation of the mind and makes us feel like meditating. The Holy Name of God that is repeated as we sip the water relieves us of all pain and sickness. Therefore, it is said in the scriptures, "Holy water is the best medicine for all ills and God is the best physician."

One should do the *ācamana* sitting. One should not talk or laugh or stand during the *ācamana*. *Ācamana* should be done pouring a spoon of water into the cavity of the right palm and sipping with devotion the holy water, chanting the mantra **Oṃ Śrī Keśavāya Svāhā**, meditating on the meaning of the mantra as, "Salutations to Lord Keśava." After sipping the holy water, one has to take the right palm over his head and bring back the palm for sipping the second time. Chanting the mantra **Oṃ Śrī Nārāyaṇāya Svāhā**, "Salutations to Lord Nārāyaṇa", one should sip the water with reverence and take the right palm above the head as before. And again one has to pour a spoon of water in the cavity of the right palm and chant **Oṃ Śrī Mādhavāya Svāhā**, "Salutations to Lord Mādhava", and do as above.

This three times sipping the water is known as *ācamana*. Now you should wash your right palm by pouring one spoon of water, chanting **Oṃ Govindāya Namaḥ**, "Salutations to Lord Govinda". Continue chanting the remaining *Caturviṁśati* i.e. 24 of the mantra-s as follows (their meanings are given below):

Oṃ Viṣṇave Namaḥ
Oṃ Madhusūdanāya Namaḥ
Oṃ Trivikramāya Namaḥ
Oṃ Vāmanāya Namaḥ
Oṃ Śrīdharāya Namaḥ
Oṃ Hṛṣīkeśāya Namaḥ
Oṃ Padmanābhāya Namaḥ
Oṃ Dāmodarāya Namaḥ
Oṃ Saṅkarṣaṇāya Namaḥ
Oṃ Vāsudevāya Namaḥ
Oṃ Pradyumnāya Namaḥ
Oṃ Aniruddhāya Namaḥ
Oṃ Puruṣottamāya Namaḥ
Oṃ Adhokṣajāya Namaḥ
Oṃ Narasiṃhāya Namaḥ
Oṃ Acyutāya Namaḥ
Oṃ Janārdanāya Namaḥ
Oṃ Upendrāya Namaḥ
Oṃ Haraye Namaḥ
Oṃ Śrīkṛṣṇāya Namaḥ

CATURVIṀŚATI-MANTRA

These 24 great mantra-s are chanted from the day of the sacred thread ceremony just before chanting the *Gāyatrī*-mantra. They are usually chanted during the early hours of the morning and in the evening when the day breaks into night. This is part of the *Sandhyā-vandanam* or salutation to God during the meeting periods of day and night. All of the twenty-four names are sacred. Taken individually, each is a great mantra, bestowing supreme powers of God. These twenty-four great names of God with the benefit therefrom are given below.

Oṃ Śrī Keśavāya Namaḥ
Oṃ Śrī Nārāyaṇāya Namaḥ

Oṃ Śrī Mādhavāya Namaḥ
Oṃ Śrī Govindāya Namaḥ
Oṃ Śrī Viṣṇave Namaḥ
Oṃ Śrī Madhusūdanāya Namaḥ
Oṃ Śrī Trivikramāya Namaḥ
Oṃ Śrī Vāmanāya Namaḥ
Oṃ Śrī Śrīdharāya Namaḥ
Oṃ Śrī Hṛṣīkeśāya Namaḥ
Oṃ Śrī Padmanābhāya Namaḥ
Oṃ Śrī Dāmodarāya Namaḥ
Oṃ Śrī Saṅkarṣaṇāya Namaḥ
Oṃ Śrī Vāsudevāya Namaḥ
Oṃ Śrī Pradyumnāya Namaḥ
Oṃ Śrī Aniruddhāya Namaḥ
Oṃ Śrī Puruṣottamāya Namaḥ
Oṃ Śrī Adhokṣajāya Namaḥ
Oṃ Śrī Narasiṁhāya Namaḥ
Oṃ Śrī Acyutāya Namaḥ
Oṃ Śrī Janārdanāya Namaḥ
Oṃ Śrī Upendrāya Namaḥ
Oṃ Śrī Haraye Namaḥ
Oṃ Śrī Kṛṣṇāya Namaḥ

TRANSLATION	BENEFIT
Salutations to Lord Keśava	Eternal wisdom
Salutations to Lord Nārāyaṇa	Final beatitude
Salutations to Lord Mādhava	Prosperity
Salutations to Lord Govinda	Obstacles removed
Salutations to Lord Viṣṇu	Cosmic consciousness
Salutations to Lord Madhusūdana	Eradication of ego
Salutations to Lord Trivikrama	Knowledge of all worlds
Salutations to Lord Vāmana	Humility and virtues
Salutations to Lord Śrīdhara	Wealth, both spiritual and material

Salutations to Lord Hṛṣīkeśa	Control of senses
Salutations to Lord Padmanābha	Realization in navel lotus
Salutations to Lord Dāmodara	Realization of the form of God
Salutations to Lord Saṅkarṣaṇa	Highest attraction
Salutations to Lord Vāsudeva	Realization of the all-pervasiveness of God
Salutations to Lord Pradyumna	Becoming son of God
Salutations to Lord Aniruddha	Light of God
Salutations to Lord Puruṣottama	Realization of the Supreme Person
Salutations to Lord Adhokṣaja	Opening of the third eye between eyebrows
Salutations to Lord Narasiṃha	Destruction of evil propensities
Salutations to Lord Acyuta	Becoming invincible
Salutations to Lord Janārdana	Seeing God in all
Salutations to Lord Upendra	Lordship
Salutations to Lord Hari	Transcendental bliss
Salutations to Lord Kṛṣṇa	Realization of Lord Kṛṣṇa

PRĀṆĀYĀMA

Prāṇāyāma or rhythmic breathing is one of the most important *kriyā*-s of Gāyatrī meditation. *Prāṇa* means breath. *Āyāma* means expansion. The discipline through which the breath is expanded is known as *prāṇāyāma*. By breath exercise, man attains longevity, health, and extraordinary energy. All ailments come to man due to lack of enough oxygen supply to all the *nāḍī*-s in the body.

Mind, breath, and semen are closely related. If one is controlled among these three, the other two are automatically controlled. By controlling the breath, the mind is brought under control and the semen or the energy is conserved. By mind control, man attains perfect consciousness and by preserving the semen, longevity, health, and creativity are gained and man is capable of helping humanity by doing noble deeds.

Deep breathing supplies enough oxygen to the lungs and the system. It purifies the blood and blesses with a healthy body. Therefore, *prāṇāyāma* should not be slighted or neglected. Everyone should practise *prāṇāyāma* regularly, every day, to keep the body and the mind healthy to carry on the duties successfully. The holy scriptures teach the method of *prāṇāyāma* as follows:

Plug the right nostril by the right thumb. Inhale the breath deeply by the left nostril until you mentally chant the *Gāyatrī*-mantra once.

Now plug both the nostrils and hold the breath until you mentally repeat the *Gāyatrī*-mantra once. Now exhale through the right nostril, plugging the left until you chant once the *Gāyatrī*-mantra.

Inhaling is known in Sanskrit as *pūraka*. Holding the breath is known as *kumbhaka*, and exhaling is khown as *recaka*. These three processes are totally known as *prāṇāyāma*. As you advance in rhythmic breathing, gradually you can increase the periods of duration by chanting three *Gāyatrī*-mantra-s while you hold the breath chanting one *Gāyatrī*-mantra during each inhalation and exhalation.

Oṃ. Praṇavasya Parabrahma ṛṣiḥ, Paramātmā devatā, Devī Gāyatrī chandaḥ. Saptānām vyāhṛtīnām Viśvāmitra-Jamadagni-Bharadvāja-Gautama-Atri-Vasiṣṭha-Kaśyapā sapta ṛṣayaḥ, Agni-Vāyu-Āditya-Bṛhaspati-Varuṇa-Indra-Viśvedevā devatāḥ. Gāyatryā Gāyatrī chandaḥ, Viśvāmitraḥ ṛṣiḥ, Savitā devatā. Śiromantrasya Parabrahma ṛṣiḥ, Paramātmā devatā, Anuṣṭup chandaḥ. Prāṇāyāme viniyogaḥ.

Parabrahma or the Transcendental Godhead Himself is the Supreme *Guru* for the *Praṇava* or *Oṃ*, the Word.

Paramātmā, the all-pervading Spirit of God, Himself is the presiding deity of this mantra; *Gāyatrī* is the meter, Viśvāmitra, Jamadagni, Bharadvāja, Gautama, Atri, Vasiṣṭha, Kaśyapa are the seers of the seven rhythms or *vyāhṛti*-s. Fire-god, wind-god, sun-god, Bṛhaspati, the celestial teacher, Varuṇa, the god of waters, Indra, the head of the celestials, and Viśvedevā or the cosmic spirit, these are the presiding deities.

For *Gāyatrī*-mantra, *Gāyatrī* itself is the meter; Viśvāmitra is the one who heard and saw this rhythm during his deep meditations; the light is God, *anuṣṭup* meter. It is prescribed for *prāṇāyāma*.

The following is muttered and meditated upon during *prāṇayāma*. The purport of the mantra-s is:

The Description of Gāyatrī Mantra

Oṃ	The word that is God
Oṃ Bhūḥ	God who is eternal
Oṃ Bhuvaḥ	God who is the creator
Oṃ Svaḥ	God who is independent
Oṃ Mahaḥ	God who is worshipful
Oṃ Janaḥ	God who has no beginning
Oṃ Tapaḥ	God who is the light of wisdom
Oṃ Satyaṃ	God who is the Truth
Oṃ Tat	That Eternal God
Savitur	That creative principle of light manifesting through the sun
Vareṇyaṃ	That Supreme God propitiated by the highest gods
Bhargo	The light that bestows wisdom, bliss, and everlasting life
Devasya	The light of that effulgent God
Dhīmahi	We meditate
Dhiyo	Intellect
Yo	Who
Naḥ	Our
Pracodayāt	May lead toward illumination
Oṃ Āpo	Oṃ. (One who protects us from) the waters (of *karma*)
Jyotiḥ	(One who is) the Light (of all the lights)
Raso	(One who is) the quintessence (in everything)
Amṛtam	(One who blesses us with) immortality
Brahma	That Almighty God

Bhūr Bhuvaḥ Svar	(Who is pervading in) earth, atmosphere, and heaven.
Oṃ	(May He bless us with enlightenment.)

The Inner Meaning

May that eternal God, our Creator, independent Reality, the worshipful, one who has no beginning, light of wisdom and Truth;

That Lord who manifests through the sun, propitiated by the highest gods, one who bestows wisdom, bliss, and everlasting life; we meditate on that Light. May our intellect be illumined by that Light of God.

One who protects us from the waters of *karma*, the Light of all the lights, the essence of everything, one who bestows immorality—May that all-pervading, almighty God bless us with enlightenment.

Saṅkalpa-kriyā

Saṅkalpa-kriyā means a total commitment to do something good. When you mentally decide that you are going to do something in the name of God at a given year, at a given month and day, at a given auspicious moment, then such a devotional commitment makes you very dear to God, who accepts your thought, word, and deed as an offering.

Usually in *Saṅkalpa-kriyā*, or the making of a noble decision for meditation, the devotee reflects on the cycles, the periods of Manu-s or Progenitors of humanity, year and solstice since the beginning of creation. This shows the remote antiquity of this creation and eternity of the soul. In the evolutionary process, which is an expansion of consciousness, one is now blessed with a human birth, a given year and a time in which one is privileged to serve the Almighty Lord to attain liberation—all these are remembered through the mantra. What a sublime *kriyā*!

A mere day of the Creator Brahmā, the son of God the Father is equal to 4,320,000,000 human years. Brahmā's night is as long as his day. His year is made up of 365 days and nights.

According to the Purāṇa-s, since this creation, Brahmā has completed fifty years of his life and the exact midday in the first day of his fifty-first year is running now. One mere day period of his is equivalent to fourteen Manu-periods. The present Manu ruling over our creation is the seventh Manu, known as Vaivasvata Manu. Now, seven is the exact half of fourteen; therefore, the almanac reads that it is the exact midday of Brahmā. It is said that when Brahmā completes his one-hundred years, he will merge in *Parabrahma*, the Father.

Now one Manu-period is approximately seventy-one great ages. Each great age is of four ages or *yuga*-s and these four *yuga*-s are known as *Kṛta Yuga*, the Golden Age; *Tretā Yuga*, the Silver Age; *Dvāpara Yuga*, the Copper Age, and *Kali Yuga*, the Iron Age.

It is known that in this Vaivasvata Manu's period, twenty-seven great ages have rolled by already and the 28th *Kali Yuga* is running right now, and this cycle (*Kalpa*, a Brahmā's day), is known as *Śveta Varāha Kalpa* or Divine Boar Cycle. In this *Kali Yuga*, which consists of 4,32,000 human years, only 5,000 years have passed until now. These are all the hidden descriptions that come in the mantra-s of *Saṅkalpa-kriyā* given below:

> Śrīmad-bhagavato mahāpuruṣasya Viṣṇor ājñayā pravartamāne adyāsmin brahmāṇḍe bhūloke Jambūdvīpe Bhārata khaṇḍe Bhārtavarṣe Meror dakṣiṇadigbhāge Brahmaṇo 'sya dvitīye parārdhe Śrī-Śvetavarāhakalpe Vaivasvata-manvantare aṣṭāviṃśatitame yuga-catuṣṭaye atra Kaliyuge prathama-caraṇe Buddhāvatāre Śālivāhanaśake vartamāne... saṃvatsare ...ayane...ṛtau...māse...pakṣe ... tithau ...vāsare evaṃguṇaviśeṣaṇaviśiṣṭāyāṃ śubhatithau mamopātta-duritakṣayadvārā śrī-Parmeśvaraprītyartham prātassandhyām upāsiṣye.

Among the endless universes created and ruled just by the mere will of Lord Viṣṇu, in this universe, on the planet earth, in *Jambū-dvīpa* (woodapple-shaped island), in the continent of King Bharata, known as *Bhāratavarṣa* (*Sanskrit* name for India), to the south of Mount Meru (considered as the axis of the universe), in the second half of the hundred years of the Creator Brahmā, in the Divine White Boar cycle, when the seventh Manu, Vaivasvata, is ruling, in this first foot of the twenty-eighth Kali Yuga, during the incarnation of the Buddha, in Śālivāhana's era, at the current year (...), solstice (...), season (...), month (...), fortnight (...), date (...), day (...), in this auspicious day characterised as above, for the destruction of all my sins committed accrued in me, towards pleasing the Supreme Lord, I shall be practising this morning meditation on *Gāyatrī* (or I am performing this *Sandhyā-vandana*).

Mārjana

Mārjana means cleansing. It is a purificatory discipline. By bathing, the body is purified, but the discipline of *mārjana* is for internal purification, which is done through mantra-s. By the discipline of *mārjana*, the flow of blood becomes rhythmic, and exciting passions subside. The Mind becomes one-pointed and meditative. Varuṇa, god of waters, becomes pleased. Meditation becomes very soothing and joyful. The unconscious and subconscious dimensions are also purified by *mārjana*. The agony of sin and ignorance is washed away. The springs of devotion manifest. The mantra of *mārjana-kriyā* runs thus:

Āpohiṣṭhetimantrasya Sindhudvīpa-Ambarīṣa ṛṣiḥ, Āpo devatā, Gāyatrī chandaḥ, mārjane viniyogaḥ.

Āpo hi ṣṭhā mayobhuvaḥ/
tā na ūrje dadhātana/
mahe raṇāya cakṣase//

yo vaḥ śivatamo rasaḥ/
tasya bhājayateha naḥ/
uśatīr iva mātaraḥ//

tasmā araṃ gamāma vaḥ/
yasya kṣayāya jinvatha/
āpo janayathā ca naḥ//

In this prayer, there are three parts. Each part is made up of three stanzas which means that there are a total of nine parts. While performing this *kriyā*, the devotee should chant all stanzas with the prefix of *Oṃ* and after chanting each stanza, he should sprinkle the water over his own head until he chants the seventh stanza. Chanting the eighth stanza, he should offer the water to the earth. Chanting the ninth stanza, once again he should sprinkle the water over his own head (*Vyāsa smṛti*).

If the *mārjana-kriyā* is done in a river, then one has to take the holy grass in one's hand to sprinkle the water on the head by chanting the mantra.

Mārjana-mantra with its nine parts is as follows. Sprinkle water on your head after you chant each mantra:

1. Oṃ. āpo hi ṣṭhā mayobhuvaḥ.
   O Water Gods, you (always) confer happiness (on those who meditate on you).
2. Oṃ. tā na ūrje dadhātana.
   Bless us with strength (to be able to do the everlasting, noble deeds).
3. Oṃ. mahe raṇāya cakṣase.
   (Bless us) to attain the highest wisdom.
4. Oṃ. yo vaḥ śivatamo rasaḥ.
   That most auspicious essence (of bliss).
5. Oṃ. tasya bhājayateha naḥ.
   Make us partakers thereof.
6. Oṃ uśatīr iva mātaraḥ.
   Even as eager mothers (feed their children with the milk from their bosom).
7. Oṃ. tasmā araṃ gamāma vaḥ.
   To him are gladly come.
   (Now offer water to the earth).
8. Oṃ. yasya kṣayāya jinvatha.
   To whose abode you send us..
9. Oṃ. āpo janayathā ca naḥ.
   Waters, Bless us with (spiritual) children (and grandchildren to continue this spiritual line).

CHART OF

Vyahṛti or Rhythm	*Tattvas or Principles*	*Tanmātra-s or Subtle Properties of Elements*	*Loka-s or Spheres*	*Devatā-s or Beings*
1. Oṃ Bhūḥ	Prithvī (Earth)	Gandha (Smell)	Earth	Indra
2. Oṃ Bhuvaḥ	Jala (Water)	Rasa (Taste)	Atmosphere	Varuṇa
3. Oṃ Svaḥ	Agni (Fire)	Rūpa (Form)	Celestial	Agni
4. Oṃ Mahaḥ	Vāyu (Air)	Sparśa (Touch)	Sphere of Saints	Vāyu
5. Oṃ Janaḥ	Ākāśa (Ether)	Śabda (Sound)	Sphere of Progenitors	Sarasvatī
6. Oṃ Tapaḥ	Mahat (Intelligence)	Buddhi (Cosmic Mind)	Sphere of the Seven Sages	Guru
7. Oṃ Satyaṃ	Puruṣa (Consciousness)	Prakṛti (Primordial Energy)	Sphere of Truth	Śiva

THE GĀYATRĪ

Vehicles	*Cakra-s or Centres of Consciousness*	*Location in the Body*	*Lotus Petals*	*Colour*
Airāvata celestial elephant (firmness and strength)	Mūlādhāra	Base of the spine	Four	Crimson
Alligator (conquering death)	Svādhiṣṭhāna	Genital	Six	Vermilion
Ram (power of quick thinking)	Maṇipūra	Navel	Ten	Blue
Black antelope (power of quick decisions)	Anāhata	Cardiac	Twelve	Red
White elephant (realization of sound and light)	Viśuddha	Cervical	Sixteen	Smoky purple
	Ājñā	Brow Centre	Two	Bright White
	Sahasrāra	Cerebrum	Thousand	Gold

Chart of the

	Musical Notes East/West		*Bija Mantra-s*	*Avasthā or State of Consciousness*	*Śakti-s or Powers*	*Prāṇa-s or Vital Airs*
1.	Sa	Do	Lam	Jāgrat or Wakeful	Ḍākinī, the power that holds earth	Vyāna (Excretory)
2.	Ri	Re	Vam	Svapna or Dream	Rākiṇī, procreative energy	Apāna (Evacuatory)
3.	Ga	Mi	Raam	Suṣupti or deep sleep	Lākinī, the digestive	Samāna (that which distributes)
4.	Ma	Fa	Yam	Turīya-Jāgrat or awakening to higher consciousness	Kākinī, respiratory	Prāṇa (Respiration)
5.	Pa	So	Ham	Turīya Svapna or mystical vision	Śākinī, speech	Udāna (Transforming Energy)
6.	Dha	La	Oṃ	Turīya-Suṣupti or Savikalpa Samādhi (Direct perception)	Hākinī, perfect thinking	Cosmic Ego
7.	Ni	Ti	Soham	Turīya-Turīya or Nirvikalpa	Śakti Kātyāyanī	Cosmic Mind

Gāyatrī

Saguṇa-Brahma or God's Manifestation	*Nirguṇa-Brahma or God as Consciousness*	*Kośa-s or Sheaths*	*Sthāna or Location in Gross Body*
Indra	All-pervading	Annamaya or Food sheath	Coccygeal
Prajāpati	Creative consciousness	Prāṇamaya or Vital sheath	Sacral
Brahmā the Creator	Wisdom consciousness	Manomaya or Mental sheath	Navel
Viṣṇu	Love	Vijñānamaya or Intellect	Cardiac
Rudra	Peace	Ānandamaya or Bliss sheath	Throat
Dakṣiṇi Mūrti or God as guru	Cosmic Consciousness	Soul	Brow
Paraśiva	Infinite Consciousness	God	Top of the brain

Āpa-prāśana-kriyā or Mantrācamana-kriyā

This is a purificatory *kriyā*. Knowingly or unknowingly, we do several errors or sins every day and night. This makes our body, mind, and word impure. Lust, anger, greediness, attachment, arrogance, and jealousy are the six enemies hidden in our psyche. By *Āpa-Prāśana* or *Mantrācamana-kriyā*, God in the solar circle purifies us.

Pour a spoonful of water in the cavity of your right palm, hold the water and chant:

> Sūryaśceti mantrasya Hiraṇyagarbha ṛṣiḥ,
> Sūrya-Manyu-Manyupati-Rātrayo devatāḥ,
> Prakṛtiḥ chandaḥ, mantrācamane viniyogaḥ.

Hiraṇyagarbha (or Brahmā Himself) is the sage for this mantra 'Sūryaśca' etc. The four presiding deities are Sūrya, Manyu, Manyupati, and Rātri. Prakṛti or the primordial energy is the metre of this mantra. It is prescribed for Mantrācamana.

Now, the following mantra is chanted to destroy all the sins of the night. Chant:

> Sūryaśca mā Manyuśca Manyupatayaśca
> manyukṛtebhyaḥ pāpebhyo rakṣantām//
> yad rātryā pāpam akārṣam
> manasā vācā hastābhyām padbhyām udareṇa siśnā/
> rātris tad avalumpatu//
> yat kiñca duritam mayi
> idam aham mām amṛtayonau/
> sūrye jyotiṣi juhomi svāhā//

(Now sip the water)

Whatever sins I did (out of anger), from those may the gods Sūrya, Manyu, and Manyupati (the angel of the day), protect me from those sins (by burning them). Whatever sins I committed through my thought, word, and hands, feet, stomach and genitals, last night, may the presiding deity over the night (Rātridevatā) destroy (those sins and protect me). Whatever the sin left in me, I offer it as an oblation in the (mystic) fire of the sun-god (so that all my sins are reduced to ash and I attain purity).

Dvitīya mārjanam (Second Purificatory Rite)

Āpohiṣṭheti navarcasya sūktasya Ambarīṣa-Sindhudvīpa ṛṣiḥ, Āpo devatā, Gāyatrī chandaḥ, pañcamī vardhamānā, saptamī pratiṣṭhā, antye dve Anuṣṭubh, mārjane viniyogaḥ.

For this hymn of nine mantra-s Ambarīṣa Sindhudvīpa is the sage. (The spirit of God manifested in) water is the deity. *Gāyatrī* is the metre. However, for the fifth mantra the metre is *Vardhamāna*; the seventh mantra is in a metre called *Pratiṣṭā*. The final two mantras are of *Anuṣṭubh* metre. It is prescribed for purification.

In *Mārjana-kriyā*, these mantra-s are used for inner purification and blessings. Now the mantra that was read before is explained here as follows·

I

Oṃ. Āpo hi ṣṭhā mayobhuvas tā na ūrje
dadhātana/
mahe raṇāya cakṣase//

(Sprinkle water on the head)
O water gods, bless us with food and happiness. Make us fit for the attainment of divine knowledge.

II

Oṃ. Yo vaḥ sivatamo rasas tasya
bhājayateha naḥ/
uśatīr iva mātaraḥ//

(Again sprinkle water on the head)
Even as the mothers feed the children with the milk of their bosom for their growth, similarly, bless us with the essence of your spirit and make us grow in God-consciousness.

III

Oṃ. Tasmā araṃ gamāma vo yasya kṣayāya
jinvatha/
āpo janayathā ca naḥ//

(Sprinkle water on the head)
We are obedient to you, O water gods. Wash our sins and inspire us to grow in spiritual realization. Also bless us with noble progeny to continue the spiritual line.

IV

Oṃ. Sanno devīr abhiṣṭaye āpo bhavantu
pītaye/
śaṃ yor abhi sravantu naḥ//

(Sprinkle water on the head)
O water gods, you have washed our sins and you have made us happy. Heal our body from all sickness and drive away all sickness from us. May we use this sanctified water for drinking and sacrificial purposes. Shower your grace upon us through these holy waters.

V

Oṃ. Īśānā vāryāṇāṃ kṣayantīś carṣaṇīnām/
āpo yācāmi bheṣajam //

(Sprinkle water on the head)
You are the bestower of material wealth and life. We pray for purity and bliss.

VI

Oṃ. Apsu me Somo abravīd antar viśvāni
bheṣajā/
Agniṃ ca viśvaśambhuvam//

(Sprinkle water on the head)

The presiding deity over the moon has told us that the holy water has all healing medicines and the mystic fire that bestows happiness.

VII

Oṃ. Āpaḥ pṛṇīta bheṣajaṃ varūtham tanve
mama/
jyok ca sūryaṃ dṛśe//

(Again sprinkle water on the head)

O gods, fill in thy life-giving waters all healing currents to keep our body immune from diseases. May we be blessed to have the *darśana* (vision) of the Lord in the region of the sun forever.

VIII

Oṃ. Idam āpaḥ pra vahata yatkiñca duritam
mayi/
yad vāham abhidudroha yad vā śepa
utānṛtam//

(Sprinkle water on the head)

O god of waters, free me from all sins that I might have committed consciously or unconsciously, by ridiculing saints or by lying. Bless me.

IX

Oṃ. Āpo adyānvacāriṣam rasena samagāsmahi/
payasvān agna āgahi tam mā saṃsṛja
varcasā//

O water gods, with a bold decision of realizing the true Self, we have come to bathe in your waters. We have bathed in your essence. O mystic fire in the waters, bless us with thy radiance.

Now chant:

Sasruṣīrityasya Āpo devatā, Anuṣṭup chandaḥ, mārjane viniyogaḥ.

For *Sasruṣir* mantra, Water spirit is the presiding deity; *Anuṣṭup* is the metre and this is used in the *Mārjana-kriyā*. Chant now:

Oṃ. Sasruṣīs tadapaso divā naktaṃ ca
sasruṣīḥ/
vareṇyakratur aham devīr avase huve//

I invoke the water-god, the fulfiller of the wishes of his devotees, with pure heart. May he bless me with pure waters to worship the supreme God day and night uninterruptedly.

Aghamarṣaṇa

Aghamarṣaṇa means that *kriyā* or discipline through which man becomes sinless. Consciously or unconsciously almost every day all people accumulate sins. The sages say that however carefully you act in the world, the sinful *karma*-s accumulated in one lifetime are enough to take us at least for fourteen more births. We accumulate as much even if we are very careful. Therefore, this *aghamarṣaṇa-kriyā* in *Gāyatrī*-mantra is one of foremost necessity in destroying sins accumulated consciously or unconsciously. A sinless mind spontaneously concentrates upon God. In *aghamarṣaṇa-kriyā*, one has to hold the breath after inhalation and lift the palm containing the little water up to the nose. One has to look into that water and should feel that all the sins are coming out of the right nostril as the power of this water enters in through the left nostril. Then without looking at the water again, one has to throw it to one's left side. The mantra to drive away all the sins from the body in this *kriyā* is as follows:

Take a spoon of water in the hand and hold it near the nose and chant:

Ṛtam ceti tṛcasya Aghamarṣaṇa ṛṣiḥ,
Bhāvavṛto devatā, Anuṣṭup chandaḥ,
pāpapuruṣavisarjane viniyogaḥ/

For the (following) three prayers 'ṛtam ca' etc., Aghamarṣaṇa is the sage (who heard these mantra-s in his meditation); God, the personal, who is pleased at the devotion of His votaries, is the presiding deity and, *Anuṣṭup* is the metre. It is prescribed for driving away the sin personified.

These mantras are chanted to throw the sinful person (*satan*) out of our body.

Now chant:

I

Oṃ. Ṛtam ca satyam cābhīddhāt
tapaso 'dhyajāyata/
tato rātryajāyata
tataḥ samudro arṇavaḥ//

II

Samudrād arṇavād adhi
saṃvatsaro 'jāyata/
ahorātrāṇi vidadhad
viśvasya miṣato vasī//

III

sūryācandramasau dhātā
yathāpūrvam akalpayat/
divaṁ ca pṛthivīṃ cāntarikṣam atho svaḥ//

Meaning in general of all three mantra-s:
(At the mere will of God) from penance the law of God (*dharma*) and Truth manifested. Then day and night, oceans, all plants, animals, and the whole creation manifested. All this is under the control of the Supreme Lord. In every cyclic beginning, God manifests the same sun, moon, heavens, atmospheric region, earth, nether regions, etc.

IV

Oṃ. Drupadād iva mumucānaḥ
svinnaḥ snātvā malād iva/
pūtam pavitreṇevājyam
āpaś śundhantu mainasaḥ//

Let this water sanctified by the mantra wash away my sins and purify me, just as a prisoner is freed from the prison house, and a man is rid of his dirt after bathing, and the *ghee* becomes an oblation by virtue of its association with ladle and fire.

After chanting the above mantra-s, you should exhale the breath from the right nostril and should feel that all of your sins have come out of the body in the form of a person. Now you should throw the water which you were holding, to your left side on the ground, feeling that the sinful person who came out of the body is destroyed. Now wash your hands and do the *ācamana* or sip the water three times.

ARGHYA-PRADĀNA

Arghya-pradāna, or pouring water oblations to the sun-god, is done to destroy a dark demon called "Sandeha", who obstructs the path of the sun. Esoterically, it means that the path of virtue is obstructed by the demon of doubt and ignorance. Therefore, the seeker of light should offer oblations to the sun-god, chanting the *Gāyatrī*-mantra which destroys the demon of darkness.

Arghya or oblation is given to the sun-god, only in a standing posture in the morning or at midday. Evening oblation is given in a sitting posture. One can offer evening oblation standing, if one is bathing in a river. Both the palms are cupped and water either from a river or from a vessel is held in the cavity of the palms and that water is offered to the sun by offering it in the river or in another vessel or on earth.

One who offers such oblations with mantra-s, both in the morning and evening, to the sun-god attains purity and illumination.

The morning oblation should be given while standing, but bending forward a little toward the sun.

Midday oblation should be given standing straight.

Evening oblation should be given seated, unless one is bathing in the river.

The water that is used for *ācamana* or sipping should not be used for oblation. Separate water should be used for *arghya* or oblation, either from a river or from a vessel.

Three oblations should be poured, chanting the *Gāyatrī*-mantra with each oblation. After that, a fourth oblation should be offered as an atonement for any fault done or any delay that was caused or for any mistakes done during this *kriyā*.

Arghya-saṅkalpa

Arghha-saṅkalpa means a commitment to offer water oblations to the sun-god. Perform one *prāṇāyāma* and do the *Arghya-saṅkalpa*.

Take a little water in the right palm and chant:

> Mamopātta-duritakṣaya-dvārā Śrī-
> Parameśvaraprītyartham prātassandhyārghya-
> pradānaṃ kariṣye.

(Offer the water on the ground)

I am offering this water during the morning *Sandhyā-vandana* for the destruction of all sins accrued in me and to please God, my Lord.

Now chant:

> Gāyatrīmantrasya Viśvāmitra ṛṣiḥ,
> Savitā devatā, Gāyatrī chandaḥ, arghya-
> pradāne viniyogaḥ.

For *Gāyatrī*-mantra, Viśvāmitra is the seer, God of Light is the presiding deity, *Gāyatrī* is the rhythm, and this is prescribed for offering oblation.

For the destruction of the demons who obstruct the path

toward the Light, three oblations are given. The first oblation is to be given after chanting the following mantra:

(Hold the water in the cavity of your palm and chant:)

Brahmāstreṇa asura-śastrārtha-nāśārtham

Oṃ. Bhūr bhuvaḥ svaḥ. Oṃ Tatsavitur
vareṇyaṁ bhargo devasya dhīmahi/
dhiyo yo naḥ pracodayāt//
Oṃ. Namo Nārāyaṇāya aruṇamaṇḍala-
madhvavartine/
Śrī Sūryanārāyaṇāya idam arghyaṃ
dattaṃ na mama.

The sense of the mantra-s is:

May the missile of *Brahmā* destroy all the weapons of the demons and may that Light of all the lights illumine my intellect. To that God, shining on the solar circle, I offer this oblation.

Now pour the first oblation. While pouring the oblation, face the sun and lift the palms containing water up to eye level. Then offer the oblation.

Again hold water in the cavity of your palm and chant:

Oṃ. Brahmadaṇḍena asuravāhana-nāśārtham

Oṃ. Bhūr bhuvaḥ svaḥ. Oṃ Tatsavitur

vareṇyaṁ bhargo devasya dhīmahi/
dhiyo yo naḥ pracodayāt//
Oṃ namo Nārāyaṇāya aruṇamaṇḍala-
madhyavartine
Śrī Sūryanārāyaṇāya idam arghyaṃ
dattaṃ na mama//

The sense of the mantra-s is:

May the staff of *Brahmā* destroy all the vehicles of the demons, and may that light of all the lights illumine my intellect. To that God, shining on the solar circle, I offer this oblation.

(Now pour the second oblation.)

Again hold water in the cavity of your palm and chant:

Brahmaśīrṣeṇa asuranāśārtham
Oṃ Bhūr bhuvaḥ svaḥ. Oṃ Tatsavitur
vareṇyaṁ bhargo devasya dhīmahi/
dhiyo yo naḥ pracodayāt//

Oṃ. namo Nārāyaṇāya aruṇamaṇḍala-
madhyavartine Śrī-Sūryanārāyaṇāya idam
arghyaṃ dattaṃ na mama.

The sense of the mantra-s is:

May the sharp weapon of *Brahmā* destroy the demons, and may that Light of all the lights illumine my intellect. To that God, shining on the solar circle, I offer this oblation.

(Now pour the third oblation)

Again hold the water in the cavity of your palm and chant:

Asuravadha-prāyaścittārtham
Oṃ Bhūr bhuvaḥ svaḥ. Oṃ Tatsavitur
vareṇyam bhargo devasya dhīmahi/
dhiyo yo naḥ pracodayāt//

Oṃ. namo Nārāyaṇāya aruṇamaṇḍala-
madhyavartine Śrī-Sūryanārāyaṇāya idam
arghyaṃ dattaṃ na mama.

The sense of these mantra-s is:

For the atonement of the sins committed by me through the destruction of the demons, I pray to that Light of lights to bless me by illumining my intellect. To that God, shining in the solar circle, I offer this oblation.

(Now pour the fouth oblation)

After the fourth oblation, touch the Mother Earth and chant:

Oṃ. Uttiṣṭha devi gantavyam
punar āgamanāya ca/
prasīda devi tuṣṭyartham
praviśya hṛdayaṃ mama//

(Saying thus, touch your bosom and chant:)

Mama hṛdaye Gāyatrīm āvāhayāmi.

The import of the mantra-s is:

O Divine Mother Gāyatrī, awake and arise. Come out of my heart to destroy the dark powers that obstruct the path of light. Then enter my heart and bless me, O blessed Mother. I invoke you to enter my heart.

(After this, chant the following:)

Oṃ Asāvādityo Brahma/

This sun is verily *Brahma*

Now hold the water in the palms as before and perambulate once and during that turning from left to right, you should sprinkle the water around. Then sit and sip the two spoons of water. That completes the *Arghya-pradāna-kriyā.* The significance of this entire *kriyā* is to remove all the impediments toward reaching the Supreme Light of Truth.

BHŪ-ŚUDDHIḤ ETC.

Bhū-śuddhi means the purification of the place where one sits for meditation. These *kriyā*-s are done to drive away the ghosts and evil spirits who may disturb our mind and meditation. That is why most of the people are not successful in their meditation. By driving the evil spirits, the meditation becomes profound and peaceful.

Now chant as follows:

Apasarpantu te bhūtā
ye bhūtā bhuvi saṃsthitāḥ/
ye bhūtā vighnakartāras-
te gacchantu śivājñayā//

Those evil spirits and ghosts who are in this place and who disturb my meditation, let them go away by the immediate order of the Supreme Lord Śiva.

Saying thus, kick the earth thrice with the hind part of the left leg.

BHŪTA-ŚUDDHIḤ

Bhūta-śuddhi is done specifically so that the ghosts and the evil spirits which are driven away should never come back again to that place to disturb the meditation.

Chant the following mantra:

Apakrāmantu bhūtāni
piśācās sarvatodiśam/

sarveṣām avirodhena
brahmakarma samārabhe//
Oṃ. Sahasrāra Huṃ Phaṭ Svāhā//

As you chant the last part of the above mantra, lift your hands above the head and clap four times on the word, *Phaṭ*. Let all the ghosts, and goblins, flee from all directions and leave this spot without any delay. I want to begin my meditation according to the *Veda*-s.

Now pray to Kṣetrapāla, the commander of the ghost-world and Śiva's attendant.

Oṃ. Tīkṣṇadaṃṣṭra mahākāya
kalpāntadahanopama/
Bhairavāya namas tubhyam
anujñām dātum arhasi//

O mountainous-bodied Kṣetrapāla of fierce tusks, like fire during the cosmic dissolution. Bhairava, salutations unto thee. Please give me permission to begin (my spiritual discipline and meditation).

Āsana-vidhi

Then one has to do the *Āsana-vidhi* or purification of the place where one sits for meditation. Spreading the holy grass on the ground, one should spread the deerskin or a mat on it. Then one should sprinkle a little holy water on that and pray to mother earth through the following mantra:

Pṛthvīmerumantrasya Merupṛṣṭha ṛṣiḥ,
Kūrmo devatā, Sutalaṃ chandaḥ, āsane
viniyogaḥ.

For Earth the mantra, Merupṛṣṭha etc., Merupṛṣṭha is the sage; Kūrma or tortoise incarnation of God is the presiding deity; Sutala is the name of the metre and is prescribed for taking the seat.

Oṃ. Pṛthvī tvayā dhṛtā lokā
devi tvam Viṣṇunā dhṛtā/
tvaṃ ca dhāraya māṃ devi
pavitraṃ kuru cāsanam//

Oṃ. O Mother Earth, the worlds are supported by you, and you are supported by Viṣṇu. O Goddess, support me too, and purify me seat.

Saying thus, one should touch and salute Mother Earth and the seat and then sit on the seat. Such a discipline is known as *Āsana-vidhi* or purifying the seat of meditation. When you sit on that sanctified seat, the divine energy, *Śakti*, is no more attracted by the gravitational pull of the earth and it takes the upward course through the spinal cord during meditation.

While you sit on that sanctified seat, you should sit either in *Padmāsana* or the Lotus posture, *Siddhāsana* or Perfect posture, or *Svastika āsana* or *Svastika* posture. You can sit cross-legged, keeping your trunk, neck, and head straight and steady. Once you sit for meditation, you should not move the limbs. Then alone can you allow the divine energy to move through the spinal cord upward, bringing spiritual experience to you. As you do the rhythmic breathing and chant the powerul mantra-s, the decaying cells of your body are divinized and the same shall be disturbed by the movement of the limbs during meditation. Therefore, on an even ground, preparing a firm seat which is neither too high nor too low, and purifying the seat as mentioned earlier, one should si+ firmly in one posture.

GĀYATRĪ-HṚDAYA

Gāyatrī-hṛdaya, or the heart of Gāyatrī.

Oṃ ityekākṣaram Brahma, Agnir devatā,
Brahma ityārṣam, Gāyatraṃ chandaḥ,
Paramātmā svarūpaṃ, sāyujye viniyogaḥ.

The monosyllabic mystical word *Oṃ* is God. God manifesting as fire is the presiding deity. *Brahma* (glorified in *Vedānta*) is the sage; *Gāyatrī* is the metre. It is of the likeness of God. It is prescribed for the highest liberation, known as *Sāyujya*.

Now, invoke and welcome Mother Gāyatrī with the following mantra:

Āyātu varadā devī
    akṣaram Brahmasammitam/
Gāyatrī chandasām mātā
    idam Brahma juṣasva me//

May Mother Gāyatrī, the fulfiller of desires, come to reveal to us the principle of Supreme Godhead as pure consciousness. May that Mother of the Veda-s and rhythms instruct us on the Brahman, the highest divine principle.

Yad ahnāt kurute pāpam
    tadahnāt pratimucyate/
yad rātryā kurute pāpam
    tad rātryā pratimucyate//

(O Universal Mother Gāyatrī, by meditating on You) one is relieved of the burden of sins he did during the day; and (one who meditates on You again) at night, that night's sins are all destroyed by You.

Sarvavarṇe mahādevi
    sandhyāvidye Sarasvati/
ajare amare devi
    sarvadevi namo 'stu te//

O Goddess Sarasvatī, (composed of) all letters, Great Goddess, esoteric worship of the twilights, never-aging, eternal, Goddess of goddesses, salutations to you.

Ojo 'si, saho 'si, balam asi, bhrājo 'si,
devānāṃ dhāma-nāmāsi, viśvaṃ asi viśvāyuḥ,
sarvam asi sarvāyur abhi bhūr Oṃ.

O Divine Mother, You are the life energy. You are the courage and prowess (with which we conquer our enemies (like ego, desire, arrogance, etc.). You are the strength (with which men carry on all duties of this and the other world). You are the shining principle. You are the Light (that makes the sun, moon, fire, and all celestial bodies shine). All forms in this universe are Your forms. You are all life. You are all. You are the life span of all (animate and inanimate objects). You are *Oṃ*.

Gāyatrīm āvāhayāmi, Sāvitrīm āvāhayāmi,
Sarasvatīm āvāhayāmi, chandarṣim āvāhayāmi,
Śriyam āvāhayāmi, balam āvāhayāmi.

The purport of the mantra-s is:
O Mother Gāyatrī, I invoke You. You are the source of all creation. I invite You to my heart. You are the embodiment of all wisdom. I welcome You, to my heart. I invoke all the metres and the sages who have seen You, to my heart. You are the wealth of the universe. I propitiate You. You are the energy in all living beings. I invite You to my heart and may my mind meditate on You, O Cosmic Mother.

(Saying thus, through the gesture of invocation, *Āvāhana-mudrā*, feel that *Gāyatrī* has entered into your body.)

Gāyatryā Gāyatrī chandaḥ, Visvāmitra
ṛṣiḥ, Savitā devatā, Agnir mukham, Brahmā
śiraḥ, Viṣṇur hṛdayam, Rudraḥ śikhā, Pṛthivī
yoniḥ, Prāṇāpānavyānodāna-samāna-saprāṇā,
śvetavarṇā, śāṇkhyāyana-sagotrā Gāyatrī
caturviṃśatyakṣarā, tripadā, ṣaṭkukṣiḥ,
pañcaśīrṣopanayane viniyogaḥ.

The sense intended is:

The presiding deity over the *Gāyatrī*-mantra has fire as Her face. Creator Brahmā is Her head. Lord Viṣṇu is Her heart. Lord Śiva is Her locks. Planet earth is Her womb. She manifests as life energy, of which the dynamic aspects are the five vital airs, known as *prāṇa*, *apāna*, *vyāna*, *udāna*, *samāna*. Also, the five sub-*prāṇas*, known as *nāga*, *kūrma*, *kṛkara*, *devadatta*, and *dhanañjaya*. It is through Her power that the five organs of perception and five organs of action are functioning. She is of white colour. The immortal Sage Śāṅkhyāyana has realized that he has his source in You. O Mother, You are of twentyfour indestructible letters, and You have *Ṛk*, *Yajus*, and *Sāma Veda*-s as Your feet. East, West, South, North, above and below, all these directions are Your stomach. The five important limbs of Veda-s, known as *Śikṣā*, *Vyākaraṇa*, *Kalpa*, *Nirukta*, and *Jyotiṣa*, these are Your five heads. Thus is the meditation on Your Cosmic Form taught during the sacred thread ceremony when the *Gāyatrī*-mantra is imparted.

GĀYATRĪ-NYĀSA

Nyāsa means location. The devotee as he meditates does the *Karanyāsa* which means touching different parts of the palm and the fingers to meditate on different planets and angels. Then there is another *nyāsa* known as *Aṅganyāsa* or location of consciousness in different parts of the body.

Nyāsa is done to feel the Divine Mother and God in the different parts of the body and make the mind concentrate on the different *cakra*-s. It is also done for the devotee to experience his spirit body or the bright body within gross body.

Nyāsa also means renunciation. Therefore, the act of renunciation is called *Sannyāsa*. Renunciation of ego or body consciousness is the goal in doing this *kriyā* known as *nyāsa*.

It is very interesting to know that our palm is the chart of our past, present, and future lives. The five fingers of the hand symbolize the five cosmic elements known as ether, air, fire, water, and earth. Spiritually speaking, the thumb always represents *Brahma*.

The index represents the ego, for it shows the world of differences by pointing out this and that, I and you. The middle finger represents *sattva-guṇa* or tranquillity. The ring finger represents *rajas* or activity and the little finger *tamas* or inactivity.

Astrologically speaking, at the base of the thumb is the mount of Venus. At the base of the index is the mount of Jupiter. At the base of the middle finger there is the mount of Saturn. And at the base of the ring finger there is the mount of Apollo. At the base of the little finger there is the mount of Mercury. Similarly, either side of the palm has Mars near the thumb, above the life line, and luna under the little finger, below the heart line. Thus the hand is the location of all the planets.

It is well-known that the brain is affecting the lines of the palm, the lines affect the brain, and the lines of the palm represent the past *karma*. The vibration of the mantra and meditation moves through the tip of the fingers. Therefore, the meditation through *karanyāsa* or hand *nyāsa* is done as a blessing to the whole of humanity, for blessings always flow from the hands of the guru.

Similarly, *aṅganyāsa* is done so that the whole body of the meditator becomes charged with divine power. Therefore, wherever such a one walks or moves, that place becomes sanctified. With this scientific background, the *nyāsa-kriyā* should be done.

Now chant:

Māṃ ca pūtaṃ kuru dhare nato 'smi tvāṃ sureśvari
āsane somamaṇḍale kūrmaskandhe upaviṣṭo 'smi.

O Mother Earth, purify me. O Great Goddess, salutations to thee. I am seated on the tortoise-seat (i.e. tortoise-shaped plank), circular like the moon.

Now chant:

Oṃ. Bhūr bhuvaḥ svar Oṃ Anantāsanāya namaḥ.

Oṃ. Bhūr bhuvaḥ svaḥ. Oṃ. Salutations to the grandseat. Saying thus, do three *prāṇāyāma*-s.

Do three more *prāṇāyāmas* and then, touching the thumb to the water, chant the following mantra. This *kriyā* is done by each of the two hands:

> Oṃ. Tat savitur, Aṅguṣṭhābhyāṃ namaḥ.

> Oṃ tat savituḥ. Salutations to that Supreme Reality represented through the two thumbs.

Touch the index with the thumb and move the thumb in a circle over the index as if God, the thumb, is humbling the ego, the index. While doing that, chant:

> Vareṇyam. Viṣṇvātmane tarjanībhyāṃ namaḥ.

> Vareṇyam. Salutations to Lord Viṣṇu who is the Supreme Lord whom I invoke in my two index fingers.

Now touch the middle finger with the thumb and move the thumb in a circle over the middle finger as you chant:

> Bhargo devasya. Rudrātmane madhyamābhyāṃ namaḥ.

> Bhargo devasya. Salutations to Rudra (Śiva) who is that shining Lord whom I invoke in the two middle fingers.

Now touch the ring finger with the thumb and move the thumb in a circle over the ring finger as you chant:

> Dhīmahi. Tattvātmane anāmikābhyāṃ namaḥ.

> Dhīamhi. Salutations to the Transcendental Principle whom I meditate on the two ring fingers.

Now touch the little finger with the thumb and move the thumb in a circle over the little finger as you chant:

> Dhiyo yo naḥ. Jñānātmane kaniṣṭhikābhyāṃ namaḥ.

> Dhiyo yo naḥ. Salutations to that Lord of wisdom whom I invoke in my two little fingers (and pray).

Now touch the right palm to the left palm and the back of the right palm to the left palm as you chant:

Pracodayāt. Sarvātmane karatalakarapṛṣṭhābhyām namaḥ.

Pracodayāt. Salutations to the all-pervading Lord whom I invoke in both sides of my two hands.

AṄGA-NYĀSA

Finally we come to the *aṅga-nyāsa* or the touching of certain locations of consciousness.

1. Touch the heart centre and chant:

Oṃ. Tatsavitur. Brahmātmane hṛdayāya namaḥ

Oṃ. Tatsavituḥ. (I meditate on that eternal Creator) Brahmā in my heart. Salutations.

2. Touch the forehead and chant:

Vareṇyam. Viṣṇvātmane śirase svāhā.

Vareṅyaṃ. (I meditate on) Lord Viṣṇu in my forehead. Salutations.

3. Touch the top of the head and chant:

Bhargo Devasya. Rudrātmane śikhāyai vaṣaṭ

Bhargo devasya. (I meditate on) Lord Rudra, aspect of Śiva, at the top of the head. Salutations.

4. Touch the right shoulder with the left hand and left shoulder with the right hand.

Dhīmahi. Tattvātmane kavacāya hum

Dhīmahi. (I meditate on) the principle of illumination that protects me as an armour. Salutations.

5. Touch the right eye.

Dhiyo yo naḥ

Dhiyo yo naḥ. (I meditate on and pray to) the illuminating principle to protect my right eye.

6. Touch the left eye.

Jñānātmane

(I meditate on and pray to) the brilliance of (the spirit to protect) my left eye.

7. Touch the centre of the brow.

Netratrayāya vauṣaṭ

(I meditate on and pray to God) to open my third eye.

8. Place both hands above the head and join the palms. On the word "*Phaṭ*", clap four times without making much sound, to drive away evil vibrations.

Pracodayāt. Sarvātmane astrāya phaṭ

Pracodayāt. (I meditate on) the all-pervading spirit to illumine me and drive away all evil.

Gāyatrī-dhyāna

Gāyatrī-dhyāna is the great meditation on *Gāyatrī*. Practice of *Gāyatrī* meditation destroys all *karma*-s and sins. By purifying the heart and the mind, it opens the third eye of illumination. Man lives long with a healthy body, shining like light and helps humanity in hastening its evolution. (For detail, refer to page 49.)

The Practice of Gāyatrī Meditation

1. The best times for the meditation are in the morning just before sunrise, and in the evening just before sunset.
2. A clean, secluded place or room should be selected for meditation.
3. One should sit for meditation facing the east in the morning, the north at noon, and the west in the evening.
4. Once you sit in a posture you should not move. As spiritual energy pervades the whole system while chanting the mantra, you should sit firmly. Keep the trunk, head, and neck erect.
5. Those who meditate on *Gāyatrī* as the Universal Mother may keep a picture of the Divine Mother and worship the Mother before and after the meditation.
6. Those who meditate on *Gāyatrī* as the Light of God can meditate on the sun-god as a symbol of light.
7. Those who meditate on the formless God may meditate on the Light of Truth in the brow centre as a flame of light.
8. While you repeat the mantra, meditate on the meaning of the mantra and pray for the vision of Mother Gāyatrī-devī.
9. The *Gāyatrī* is a cosmic rhythm consisting of twenty-four syllables arranged as a triplet of eight syllables each.
10. The *Ṛg Vedic Gāyatrī*-mantra is a prayer for light, for illumination.

The Description of Gāyatrī-mantra

Oṃ	The word that is God
Bhūḥ	God who is eternal
Oṃ Bhuvaḥ	God who is the creator
Oṃ Svaḥ	God who is independent
Oṃ Mahaḥ	God who is worshipful
Oṃ Janaḥ	God who has no beginning
Oṃ Tapaḥ	God who is the light of wisdom
Oṃ Satyam	God who is the Truth
Oṃ Tat	That Eternal God
Savitur	Of that creative principle of light manifesting through the sun

Vareṇyam	That Supreme God propitiated by the highest gods
Bhargo	The light that bestows wisdom, bliss, and everlasting life
Devasya	The light of that effulgent God
Dhīmahi	We meditate
Dhiyo	Our intellect
Yo	Who
Naḥ	Our
Pracodayāt	May lead toward illumination
Oṃ Āpo	Oṃ (One who protects us from) the waters (of *karma*)
Jyotī	(One who is) the Light (of all the lights)
Raso	(One who is) the quintessence (in everything)
Oṃ ṛtam	(One who blesses us with) immortality
Brahma	That Almighty God
Bhūr Bhuvaḥ Svar	(Who is pervading in) earth, atmosphere, and heaven
Oṃ	(May He bless us with enlightenment)

The Inner Meaning

May that eternal God, our Creator, independent Reality, the worshipful, one who has no beginning, light of wisdom, and Truth.

That Lord who manifests through the sun, propitiated by the highest gods, one who bestows wisdom, bliss, and everlasting life—we meditate on that Light. May our intellect be illumined by that Light of God.

One who protects us from the waters of *karma*, the Light of all the lights, the essence of everything, one who bestows immortality—May that all-pervading almighty God bless us with enlightenment.

KRIYĀ-S (Actions)

The Gāyatrī mantra

Oṃ Bhūḥ:
(Touch the thumb to the base of the ring finger.)
Oṃ Bhuvaḥ:
(Touch the thumb to the base of the little finger.)
Oṃ Svaḥ.
(Touch the thumb to the middle of the little finger.)
Oṃ Mahaḥ:
(Touch the thumb to the tip of the little finger.)
Oṃ Janaḥ:
(Touch the thumb to the tip of the ring finger.)
Oṃ Tapaḥ:
(Touch the thumb to the tip of the middle finger.)
Oṃ Satyam:
(Touch the thumb to the tip of the index finger.)
Oṃ Tatsavitur Vareṇyam:
(Touch the thumb to the middle of the index finger.)
Bhargo Devasya Dhīmahi:
(Touch the thumb to the base of the index finger.)
Dhiyo Yo Naḥ Pracodayāt:
(Touch the thumb to the base of the middle finger.)
Oṃ Āpo Jyotiḥ:
(Touch three fingers of the right hand to the right eye.)
Raso'mṛtam:
(Touch three fingers of the right hand to the left eye.)
Brahma Bhūr Bhuvaḥ Svar Oṃ:
(Touch three fingers of the right hand to the third eye.)

PRACTICE

Chant this mantra with the *kriyā*-s three times. Chant the mantra seven more times without the *kriyā*. Those who practise intense meditation could go up to 108 to 1008 *Gāyatrī*-s.

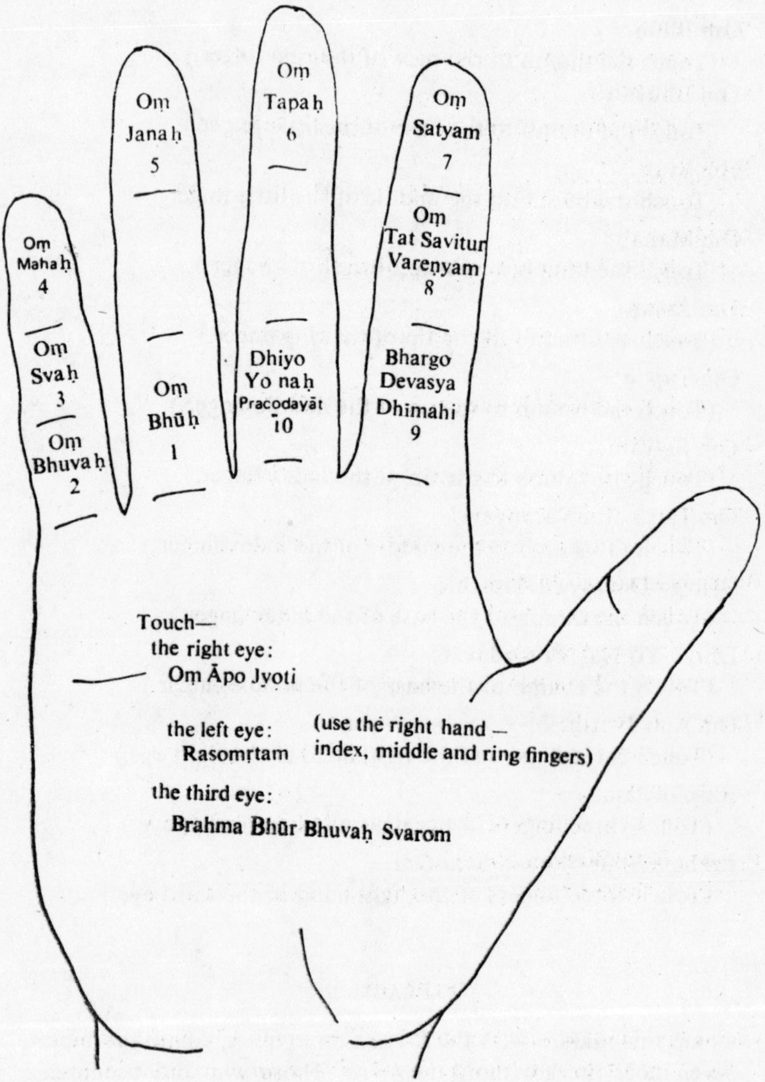

Oṃ
Tapaḥ
6
Oṃ
Janaḥ
5
Oṃ
Satyam
7
Oṃ
Mahaḥ
4
Oṃ
Tat Savitur
Vareṇyam
8
Oṃ
Svaḥ
3
Oṃ
Bhūḥ
1
Dhiyo
Yo naḥ
Pracodayāt
10
Bhargo
Devasya
Dhimahi
9
Oṃ
Bhuvaḥ
2
Touch—
the right eye:
Oṃ Āpo Jyoti
the left eye:
Rasomṛtam
(use the right hand —
index, middle and ring fingers)
the third eye:
Brahma Bhūr Bhuvaḥ Svarom

GĀYATRĪ-JAPA-SAṄKALPA

Gāyatrī-japa-saṅkalpa means deciding that you are going to chant the *Gāyatrī*-mantra 108 times, 1,008 times, 28 times, or at least 10 times.

Begin by chanting the following mantra:

> Mamopātta-duritakṣayadvārā Śrī-
> Parameśvaraprītyartham yathāśakti Gāyatrī-
> japaṃ kariṣye.

For the eradication of all sinful *karma*-s, that have accrued in me, I repeat the *Gāyatrī*-mantra according to my capacity, to please my Lord.

Chant the short version of the *Gāyatrī*-mantra:

> Oṃ. Bhūr bhuvaḥ svaḥ.
> Oṃ. Tat savitur vareṇyam
> Bhargo devasya dhīmahi/
> Dhiyo yo naḥ pracodayāt//

The purport is:

O effulgent light that has given birth to all the *loka*-s or spheres of consciousness, O God who appears through the shining sun, illumine our intellect.

This is the surface meaning of the text. In this short version of *Gāyatrī*-mantra, *Oṃ* symbolizes God, *Bhūḥ* represents earth, *Bhuvaḥ* represents the atmospheric regions, covering all the subdivisions of semigods and demigods up to the sun. *Svaḥ* represents the third dimension or celestial region, known as *Svarga-loka* and all the luminous *loka*-s above.

Finish your meditation by chanting the following mantra:

> Yathāśakti Gāyatrī-japārādhanena
> sarvātmakaḥ Śrī-Parameśvaraḥ prīyatām/
> Prīto varado bhavatu//

By the *japa* I did according to my capacity (to the all-pervading Lord of the universe). May the Lord be pleased. And, thus pleased may He bless me.

Mantra and Silence

Again chant the *Gāyatrī*-mantra as above (without *kriyā*-s) and enter into deep silence. This is the great prayer for the opening of the third eye, for illumination, for Christ-consciousness.

After the silence, before you get up, repeat this: *Oṃ Śāntiḥ, Śāntiḥ, Śāntiḥ* for peace above, peace within, and peace to all beings.

May the Holy Gāyatrī and all the prophets and sages protect you, guide you, and lead you gently to reach the highest illumination.

TARPAṆA

Tarpaṇa-kriyā is water offering to the chosen deity or ancestors. At the outset make the assertion:

Prātassandhyā-tarpaṇam kariṣye/

I am going to make the morning-offering of water.

Pour water in the cavity of the cupped right palm and offer the holy water down the tip of the fingers to propitiate the four aspects of the *Gāyatrī* light as you chant:

1. Sandhyāṃ tarpayāmi
   I propitiate the power of the dawn and dusk.
2. Gāyatrīṃ tarpayāmi
   I propitiate the *Gāyatrī*, the Light of Truth.
3. Brāhmīṃ tarpayāmi
   I propitiate the *Brāhmī*, the power of Brahmā.
4. Nirmṛjīṃ tarpayāmi
   I propitiate the Power of God that blesses with immortality.

UPASTHĀNA

Upasthāna-kriyā forms the prayers offered to the sun-god, fire-god, and other deities of light.

Join the palms and chant the prayers as follows:

Mitrasyeti catasṛṇāṃ Viśvāmitra ṛṣiḥ, Mitro devatā,
Gāyatrī chandaḥ, Sūryopāsane viniyogaḥ/

Sage Viśvāmitra is the seer of this mantra of four verses beginning with (the word) Mitrasya; Mitra is the presiding deity; *Gāyatrī* is the metre. Such is the affirmation in this *Upasthāna-kriyā* of the sun.

I

Oṃ. Mitrasya carṣaṇīdhṛtaḥ
Śravo devasya sānasim/
Dyumnam citraśravastamam//

It is by the light and blessings of the sun-god that we are blessed with food, wealth, and life. (Salutations)

II

Oṃ. Abhi yo mahinā divaṁ
Mitro babhūva saprathāḥ/
Abhi śravobhiḥ pṛthivīm//

Oṃ. The all-pervading Light of the Lord manifesting through the sun blesses us with timely rain and food for everybody.

III

Oṃ. Mitrāya pañca yemire
Janā abhiṣṭiśavase/
Sa devān viśvān bibhrati//

Oṃ. All the sages offer their oblations to that Light of the sun-god that has the prowess to vanquish the dark powers.

IV

Oṃ. Mitro deveṣvāyuṣu
Janāya vṛkta barhiṣe/
Iṣa iṣṭavratā skaḥ//

Oṃ. Āditya, the sun-god, fulfils the desires and blesses with plenty that devotee who offers oblations to him.

Oṃ. Jātavedase ityasya mantrasya Kaśyapa ṛṣiḥ, Triṣṭup chandaḥ, Jātavedā Agnir devatā, Agnyupasthāne viniyogaḥ/

Sage Kaśyapa is the seer for this mantra beginning with (the word) Jātavedase; Triṣṭup is the metre; Mystic fire is the presiding deity. Such is the affirmation of this *upasthāna-kriyā* of Fire.

Oṃ. Jātavedase sunavāma soma-
marātīyato ni dahāti vedaḥ/
sa naḥ parṣadati durgāṇi viśvā
nāveva sindhum duritātyagniḥ//

Oṃ. May the mystic fire destroy the evil powers. Even as a boat-man takes us across on his boat, similarly, may the mystic fire take us across the ocean of grief and sins. May we attain peace.

Oṃ. Tryambakam ityasya Vasiṣṭha ṛṣiḥ, Anuṣṭup chandaḥ, Tryambaka-Rudro devatā, upasthāne viniyogaḥ/

Oṃ. Sage Vasiṣṭha is the seer of this mantra beginning with (the word) Tryambakam. *Anuṣṭup* is the metre. Three-eyed Śiva is the presiding deity. This is the affirmation of *upasthāna-kriyā.*

Oṃ. Tryambakam yajāmahe
sugandhim puṣṭivardhanam/
urvārukam iva bandhanāt
mṛtyor mukṣyeta nānṛtāt//

Oṃ. May that three-eyed Lord of eternal fragrance of fame bless us with prosperity, longevity, and health. Let him sever us from the clutches of death, even as a cucumber from its creeper. (Let him not sever us) from immortality.

Oṃ. Tacchaṃyor ityasya mantrasya Śaṃyu ṛṣiḥ, Śakvarī chandaḥ, Viśvedevā devatāḥ, śāntyarthe jape viniyogaḥ/

Oṃ. For this metre, beginning with the word Tacchaṃyoḥ Sage Śaṃyu is the seer. *Śakvarī* is the metre. *Viśvadevā* or cosmic spirits are the presiding deities; for everlasting peace is this affirmation.

Oṃ. Tacchaṃyor ā vṛṇīmahe
gātuṃ yajñāya gātuṃ yajñapataye/
daivī svastir astu naḥ/
svastir mānuṣebhyaḥ/
ūrdhvam jigātu bheṣajam//
Śanno astu dvipade śaṃ catuṣpade//
Oṃ Śāntiḥ Śāntiḥ Śāntiḥ

Oṃ. O God, we pray for transcendental peace untouched by misery. We pray for health and happiness to sing the Veda at the sacrifices and to the Lord of sacrifices. May all divine blessings come upon us. May all men attain happiness by the grace of the Lord. May we enjoy healing (and health). May all animals be happy. Oṃ Peace, Peace, Peace.

Oṃ. Namo Brahmaṇe namo astvagnaye, namaḥ Pṛthivyai, nama oṣadhībhyaḥ, namo Vāce, namo Vācaspataye, namo Viṣṇave, mahate karomi Brahma, Bhūr bhuvaḥ svar Oṃ Śāntiḥ Śāntiḥ Śāntiḥ

Salutations to Brahmā. Salutations to Agni, the fire-god. Salutations to Mother Earth. Salutations to the plant kingdom. Salutations to Goddess Sarasvatī. Salutations to Creator Brahmā. Salutation to Lord Viṣṇu. Salutations again and again to Gāyatrī. Oṃ, peace, peace, peace.

Oṃ. Indrāya namaḥ	Salutation to Indra, the Lord of the first heaven.
Oṃ. Agnaye namaḥ	Salutation to Agni, the Fire-god.
Oṃ. Yamāya namaḥ	Salutation to Yama, the god of Death.

Oṃ. Nirṛtaye namaḥ	Salutation to Nirṛti, the shining one.
Oṃ. Varuṇāya namaḥ	Salutation to Varuṇa, the god of waters.
Oṃ. Vāyave namaḥ	Salutation to Vāyu, the Wind god.
Oṃ. Kuberāya namaḥ	Salutation to Kubera, the god of wealth.
Oṃ. Īśānāya namaḥ	Salutation to Īśāna, the Lord Śiva.

Now you should utter the name of your *gotra* or lineage. Then chant:

Yāṃ sadā sarvabhūtāni
sthāvarāṇi carāṇi ca/
sāyaṃ prātar namasyanti
sā mā Sandhyābhirakṣatu// Oṃ namaḥ.

The sense is:

Salutation to the Universal Mother, Sandhyā Devī, who is worshipped by all the angels, animate and inanimate objects, and sages and saints at dawn and dusk.

Gāyatrī-prasthāpana

Now, fold your hands and pray:

Oṃ. Uttame śikhare jāte
bhūmyām parvatamūrdhani/
brāhmaṇebhyo 'bhyanujñātā
gaccha devi yathāsukham//

The sense is:

O Eternal Mother, Gāyatrī-devī, those who were meditating on You are praying to You reverentially that You may return to Your divine abode in the central peak of the Meru Mountain.

Stutā mayā varadā devamātā
pracodayantāṃ pāvamānī dvijānām/
āyuḥ prāṇaṃ prajāṃ paśuṃ
kīrtiṃ draviṇaṃ brahmavarcasam/
mahyaṃ datvā vrajata brahmalokam//

This means:

O Mother of the Veda-s, Gāyatrī devī, one who is inspiring all beings, remaining as an indwelling spirit in every heart, You are the power of *Parabrahman* and manifest in the solar circle. Bless us with health and longevity, wealth, and spiritual brilliance. Return to Thy abode, from where You have come to give us *darśana*. Salutations.

Now do the *ācamana* or sip the water thrice; do the *prāṇāyāma* and chant:

Mamopātta-duritakṣayadvārā Śrī-Parameśvaraprītaye prātaḥkāla-sandhyā-vandanena bhagavān sarvātmakaḥ Śrī-Parameśvaraḥ prīyatām/

The sense is:

May this morning meditation destroy all my sins and may my Lord be pleased.

Now chant:

Mantrahīnaṃ kriyāhīnaṃ bhaktihīnaṃ ramāpate/
yatkṛtaṃ tu mayā deva paripūrṇaṃ tad astu te//

Anena prātassandhyāvandanena bhagavān Savitṛ-nāmakaḥ Śrī-Mahāviṣṇuḥ prīyatām. Prīto bhavatu. Śrī-Kṛṣṇārpaṇam astu/

This prayer states:

My Lord, there may be many mistakes in my intonation of the mantra. I know not any *kriyā* and I am lacking in true devotion. O Perfect Lord, make my imperfect meditation perfect. Thus I have performed my morning *Sandhyā-vandana* by propitiating God through the circle of the sun. May Heavenly Father Mahāviṣṇu be pleased with my devotion. I offer this prayer and meditation to Lord Śrī Kṛṣṇa.

Hari Oṃ Tat Sat
Oṃ Śāntiḥ Śāntiḥ Śāntiḥ.

MIDDAY SANDHYĀ-VANDANA

FOR THE MIDDAY and evening *Sandhyā-vandana*, most of the mantra-s and *kriyā*-s are the same as for the morning *Sandhyā-vandana*. Only a few mantra-s differ in *Saṅkalpa-kriyā* (decision to meditate), *Ap-prāśana* (sipping of water), *Arghya-pradāna* (pouring oblations), *Upasthāna* (special prayer), and *Tarpaṇa* (water offering). For the mantra-s only the general sense is given.

For the midday meditation, during *Saṅkalpa*, you should chant:

Mādhyāhnikaṃ sandhyopāstim kariṣye/

I am hereby conducting my midday meditation on Light.

During the *Ap-prāśana-kriyā*, the following mantra is to be chanted:

Āpaḥ punantvityasya Nārāyaṇa ṛṣiḥ, aṣṭi chandaḥ, Āpo devatā, antaḥśuddhyartham ap-prāśane viniyogaḥ/

For this mantra, Lord Nārāyaṇa is the sage. *Aṣṭi* is the name of the metre. Holy waters are the deities. This is done for inner purification. Such is the affirmation.

Now chant:

Oṃ. Āpaḥ punantu pṛthivīm
pṛthivī pūtā punātu mām/
punantu Brahmaṇaspatir
Brahma putā punātu mām/

yad ucchiṣṭam abhojyam
yad vā duścaritam mama/
sarvam punantu mām āpo
asatām ca pratigraham // svāhā//

May the waters purify the Mother Earth. May the purified Earth purify me. May the Waters purify the teacher of the Veda-s. May the wisdom of the teacher purify me. May the Waters purify me from the sins which I might have committed by eating things which are forbidden by the scriptures, for evil actions committed, or for receiving gifts earned through sinful methods. Yea, may the waters purify me.

For the midday *Sandhyā-vandana*, the following mantra should be chanted in *Arghya-pradāna-kriyā*, offering oblations to the sun-god.

Oṃ. Namo Nārāyaṇāya. Madhyāhne Bhāskara-maṇḍala-madhyavartine Śrī-Sūryāya idam arghyam/

I offer this midday oblation to the Supreme Lord who is manifesting in the middle of the solar circle.

As in the morning oblation, you chant the *Gāyatrī*-mantra and pour oblations to the sun.
Now offer this special prayer to the sun-god:

Udutyam ityasya Praskaṇva ṛṣiḥ, Sūryo devatā, Gāyatrī chandaḥ, upasthāne viniyogaḥ.

For this mantra, Sage Praskaṇva is the seer, sun is the deity, *Anuṣṭup* is the metre; to cure all diseases this prayer is sung and such is the affirmation.

Oṃ. Udu tyaṃ jātavedasam
devaṃ vahanti ketavaḥ/
dṛśe viśvāya sūryam//

O sun-god, to shower your blessings upon the earth, your seven celestial horses pull your chariot above in the sky.

Udyannadyeti tṛcasya Praskaṇva ṛṣiḥ, Sūryo devatā, Anuṣṭup chandaḥ, sakalaroga-sāntyarthe viniyogaḥ/

For the three following mantras Sage Praskaṇva is the seer, sun is the deity, *Anuṣṭup* is the metre. For the cure of all diseases, these mantra-s are chanted; such is the affirmation.

I

Oṃ. Udyannadya Mitramaha
ārohann uttarāṃ divam/
hṛdrogam mama Sūrya
harimāṇam ca nāśaya//

O friend of the universe, O shining Lord of the solar circle, kindly relieve me of my physical sickness and mental worries. Bless me with peace.

II

Oṃ. Śukeṣu me harimāṇam
ropaṇākāsu dadhmasi/
atho hāridraveṣu me
harimāṇam nidadhmasi//

O sun-god, keep the colour of my body healthy. May any colour that destroys the health not come to me. Let that colour remain with those objects where it shines.

III

Oṃ. Udagād ayam Ādityo
viśvena sahasā saha/
dviṣantam mahyaṃ randhayan
mo aham dviṣate radham//

O sun-god, you have risen with great glory after destroying all my sickness. Salutations!

Now about *Tarpaṇa*-mantra for midday meditation. Oblations are poured to four deities as below:

1. Oṃ. Sandhyāṃ tarpayāmi
   To the deity of dawn and dusk I pour oblations.
2. Oṃ. Sāvitrīṃ tarpayāmi
   To the Light of God I pour oblations.
3. Oṃ. Vaiṣṇavīṃ tarpayāmi
   To the power of Viṣṇu I pour oblations.
4. Oṃ. Nirmṛjīṃ tarpayāmi
   To the life-giving power I pour oblations.

All the rest of the *kriyā*-s are just as in the morning.

Evening Sandhyā-vandana

In the evening, *Sandhyā-vandana* mantra-s differ only in *Ap-prāśana*, *Arghya-pradāna*, *Tarpaṇa*, and *Upasthāna-kriyā*-s. All the rest of the *kriyā*-s and mantra-s are the same as in the morning *Sandhyā-vandana*.

When you perform evening *Sandhyā-vandana* during *Saṅkalpa-kriyā* chant:

Sāyaṃsandhyāvandanam ahaṃ kariṣye/

I am taking the decision to perform the evening *Sandhyā-vandana*.

For *Ap-prāśana-kriyā*, chant the following mantra:

Agniścetyasya mantrasya Yājñavalkyopaniṣada ṛṣiḥ, Agni-Manyu-Manyupatayo devatāḥ, Prakṛtiś chandaḥ, antaḥ-śuddhyartham ap-prāśane viniyogaḥ/

For this mantra, Sage Yājñavalkya is the seer. Fire-god, Manyu, and Manyupati are the deities. *Prakṛti* is the metre.

For inner purification, these mantra-s are chanted and this is the affirmation.

Oṃ. Agniś ca mā Manyuś ca Manyupatayaś ca manyukṛtebhyaḥ pāpebhyo rakṣantām/ yad ahnā pāpam akārṣam manasā vācā hastābhyāṃ padbhyāṃ udareṇa śiśnā ahas tad avalumpatu. Yatkiñca duritam mayi idam ahaṃ satye jyotiṣi juhomi svāhā/

May the fire-god destroy my sins done due to anger. May the presiding deity over the night destroy any sins I have committed through thought, word, or deed; or through food, sex, or any reasons. I offer all my bad *karma*-s in the mystic fire of *Brahmā*. May I be purified.

During the *Tarpaṇa-kriyā* in the evening, pour oblations to the four deities as follows:

1. Oṃ. Sandhyāṃ tarpayāmi
   I offer oblations to the deity of dawn and dusk.
2. Oṃ. Sarasvatīṃ tarpayāmi
   I offer oblations to Goddess Sarasvatī.
3. Oṃ. Raudrīṃ tarpayāmi
   I offer oblations to Goddess Raudrī, the spouse of Rudra or Śiva.
4. Oṃ. Nirmṛjiṃ tarpayāmi
   I offer oblations to the life-giving power of God.

Now, in the *Upasthāna-kriyā* for the evening, the following mantra-s are to be chanted:

Yacchiddhi ta iti pañcarcasya Śunaḥśepa ṛṣiḥ, Varuṇo devatā, Gāyatrī chandaḥ, upasthāne viniyogaḥ/

For these mantras, Sage Śunaḥśepa is the seer; Varuṇa is the presiding deity; *Gāyatrī* is the metre; and this is used in the *Upasthāna-kriyā*.

The following is the prayer to Varuṇa, the god of Waters, in the *Upasthāna-kriyā*:

I

Oṃ. Yacchiddhi te viśo yathā
pra deva Varuṇa vratam/
minīmasi dyavi dyavi//

O Varuṇa, due to negligence, we have not offered our worship to you. Please forgive us and give us the blessings to propitiate you.

II

Oṃ. Mā no vadhāya hatnave
jihilanasya rīradhaḥ/
mā hṛṇānasya manyave//

(O Varuṇa), do not punish us for this negligence. Do not be angry with us. Bless us to propitiate you.

III

Oṃ. Vi Mṛlīkāya te mano
rathīr aśvam na sanditam/
gīrbhir Varuṇa sīmahi//

O Varuṇa, be pleased by our prayers to you, even as the tired horses are pleased by the food offered by the charioteer.

IV

Oṃ. Parā me vimanyavaḥ
patanti vasya iṣṭaye/
vayo na vasatīr upa//

O Varuṇa, my mind which was extroverted turns within my heart for meditation, even as the birds return to their nests.

V

Oṃ. Kadā kṣatraśriyam naramā
Varuṇam karāmahe/
Mṛlīkāyor ucakṣasam//

O Varuṇa, you are the all-knowing, all-powerful Lord. We propitiate you. Come to us, O Lord, bless us with peace and happiness.

Oṃ. Śāntiḥ Śāntiḥ Śāntiḥ

May the entire world be filled with peace.

Here ends the evening *Sandhyā-Vandana*. May Gāyatrī-devī bless all with illumination.

MEDITATION ON KUṆḌALINĪ THROUGH THE GĀYATRĪ MANTRA

THERE ARE seven *vyāhṛti*-s, or rhythms, in the *Gāyatrī*-mantra. They are: *Oṃ Bhūḥ, Oṃ Bhuvaḥ, Oṃ Svaḥ, Oṃ Mahaḥ, Oṃ Janaḥ, Oṃ Tapaḥ*, and *Oṃ Satyam*. The aspirant should practise the discipline in the following way to awaken the *Śakti*:

Sit in *Padmāsana* (lotus posture) or *Siddhāsana* (adept's posture), facing East or North.

1. Close your eyes and meditate on *mūlādhāra-cakra* at the base of the spine and inhale. Visualize the four-petalled lotus there while you retain the breath. As you exhale, chant "*Oṃ Bhūḥ*".
2. Feel that the *śakti* is awakened and reaches the *svādhiṣṭhāna-cakra*, the genital centre. Inhale, and as you hold the breath in, meditate on the six-petalled lotus. As you exhale, chant "*Oṃ Bhuvaḥ*".
3. Now feel that the *śakti* has entered into the *maṇipūra-cakra*, the navel centre. As you inhale, and retain the breath, meditate on the ten-petalled lotus. As you exhale, chant "*Oṃ Svaḥ*".
4. Now the Divine *Śakti* pierces the fourth *cakra*, known as the *anāhata-cakra*, the cardiac centre. Inhale deeply and meditate on the twelve-petalled lotus as you hold the breath, and chant "*Oṃ Mahaḥ*" as you exhale.
5. As the Divine Śakti enters the *viśuddha-cakra* of sixteen petals at the throat centre, inhale and meditate on that *cakra* while holding the breath, and chant "*Oṃ Janaḥ*" as you exhale.

6. Now your meditation should be on the brow centre known as *ājñā-cakra*, a lotus with two petals. It is the third eye centre. Meditate on Divine Śakti in the *cakra* as you inhale and retain the breath. As you exhale, chant "*Oṃ Tapaḥ*".
7. Inhale and retain the breath; meditate as above and as you exhale, chant "*Dhiyo yo naḥ pracodayāt*" (illumine our intellect).

Sit in silent meditation for some time. Then feel that you are bringing the Divine Śakti back to Her abode at the base of the spine. Chant "*Oṃ*" and feel that She is returning to the brow centre from the thousand-petalled lotus. Now chant "*Ham*" and feel that She has come to the throat centre. "*Yam*" is the mantra you should chant as She returns to the cardiac centre. With the mantra "*Ram*" you should propitiate Her in the navel centre. Goddess Śakti sprinkles the divine nectar throughout the body as She returns to Her original seat. Chant "*Vam*" as She comes to the genital centre. Finally, chant "*Lam*" when She returns to the *mūlādhāra cakra*.

Again sit in silent meditation for a few minutes. Take a deep breath, pray for universal peace and, as you exhale, chant "*Oṃ Śāntiḥ*". You will attain the peace that passeth all understanding.

DIFFERENT GĀYATRĪ-S

AS THE *Vaidika Gāyatrī*, that is *Oṃ Bhūr Bhuvaḥ Svaḥ*; *Oṃ Tat Savitur Vareṇyam*; *Bhargo Devasya Dhīmahi*; *Dhiyo Yo naḥ Pracodayāt*, became universally known as the greatest mantra, the Himalayan masters composed similar prayers with the same *Gāyatrī* meter on other important aspects of God's manifestations. This helped many people who wanted to propitiate those aspects of God. Here, the *Gāyatrī* means the prosody or the metre in which these prayers were written. Twenty such prayers on different aspects of God are given below with the meanings implied.

1. *Gaṇeśa-Gāyatrī*

Oṃ. Ekadantāya vidmahe
Vakratuṇḍāya dhīmahi/
Tanno dantiḥ pracodayāt//

May we realize Lord Gaṇeśa. Let us meditate on that elephant-headed god who removes the hurdles. May that one-tusked god enlighten us (one tusk symbolizes the oneness).

2. *Narasiṃha-Gāyatrī*

Oṃ. Vajranakhāya vidmahe
Tīkṣṇadaṃṣṭrāya dhīmahi/
Tanno Narasiṃhaḥ pracodayāt//

May we realize Narasiṃha, the man-lion god, with his diamond nails that pierce the veil of ignorance. Let us meditate on that sharp-toothed one that destroys the demon of darkness. May that Lord Narasiṃha illumine us.

3. *Nārāyaṇa-Gāyatrī*

Oṃ. Nārāyaṇāya vidmahe
Vāsudevāya dhīmahi/
Tanno Viṣṇuḥ pracodayāt//

May we realize Lord Nārāyaṇa, the Heavenly Father. Let us meditate on his Vāsudeva aspect (indwelling spirit in all). May that Lord Viṣṇu illumine us.

4. *Mahālakṣmī-Gāyatrī*

Oṃ. Mahālakṣmī ca vidmahe
Viṣṇupatnī ca dhīmahi/
Tanno Lakṣmī pracodayāt//

May we realize Mahālakṣmī. Let us meditate on that spouse of Lord Viṣṇu and may Goddess Lakṣmī illumine us.

5. *Kālī* or *Devī-Gāyatrī*

Oṃ. Ādyāyai vidmahe
Parameśvaryai dhīmahi/
Tanno Kālī pracodayāt//

May we realize the Primordial Energy. Let us meditate on that Parmeśvarī, the spouse of Śiva. May that Goddess Kālī illumine us.

6. *Brahma-Gāyatrī*

Oṃ. Parameśvarāya vidmahe
Paratattvāya dhīmahi/
Tanno Brahmā pracodayāt//

May we realize the Supreme Brahma. Let us meditate on that transcendental principle and may God Brahmā illumine us.

7. *Haṃsa-Gāyatrī*

Oṃ. Haṃsāya vidmahe
Paramahaṃsāya dhīmahi/
Tanno Haṃsaḥ pracodayāt//

May we realize *Haṃsa* that is our own Self as swan. Let us meditate on that *Paramahaṃsa*, the Supreme Self. May Haṃsa illumine us.

8. *Agni-Gāyatrī*

Oṃ. Vaiśvānarāya vidmahe
Lālelāya dhīmahi/
Tanno Agniḥ pracodayāt//

May we realize Vaiśvānara, the fire-god. Let us meditate on that seven-tongued, mystic fire and may that Agni, the fire-god, illumine us.

9. *Sūrya-Gāyatrī*

Oṃ. Bhāskarāya vidmahe
Divākarāya dhīmahi/
Tanno Sūryaḥ pracodayāt//

May we realize Bhāskara, the shining one. Let us meditate on that Divākara, the presiding deity over the day, and may that Sūrya, the sun-god, illumine us.

10. *Durgā-Gāyatrī*

Oṃ. Kātyāyanyai ca vidmahe
Kanyākumāryai ca dhīmahi/
Tanno Durgā pracodayāt//

May we realize Kātyāyanī, the Śakti. Let us meditate on Kanyākumarī, the virgin goddess. And may that Durgā, illumine us.

11. *Hiraṇyagarbha-Gāyatrī*

Oṃ. Vedātmane vidmahe
Hiraṇyagarbhāya dhīmahi/
Tanno Brahmā pracodayāt//

May we realize the spirit of the Vedas. Let us meditate on that Hiraṇyagarbha, the golden-wombed god. May that Creator Brahmā illumine us.

12. *Rudra-Gāyatrī*

Oṃ. Tatpuruṣāya vidmahe
Mahādevāya dhīmahi/
Tanno Rudraḥ pracodayāt//

May we realize the *Tatpuruṣa*, the Transcendental Person. May we meditate on that Mahādeva, the greatest god, and may that Rudra illumine us.

13. *Āditya-Gāyatrī*

Oṃ. Divākarāya vidmahe
Prabhākarāya dhīmahi/
Tanno Ādityaḥ pracodayāt//

May we realize the Light of God, Divākara. Let us meditate on the shining principle, Prabhākara, and may that sun-god, Āditya, illumine us.

14. *Garuḍa-Gāyatrī*

Oṃ. Tatpuruṣāya vidmahe
Suvarṇapakṣāya vidmahe/
Tanno Garuḍaḥ pracodayāt//

May we realize that *Tatpuruṣa*, the Supreme Principle. Let us meditate on His vehicle, the golden-winged eagle and may that Garuḍa illumine us.

15. *Nandī-Gāyatrī*

Oṃ. Tatpuruṣāya vidmahe
Cakratuṇḍāya dhīmahi/
Tanno Nandī pracodayāt//

May we realize that *Tatpuruṣa,* the Transcendental Power. Let us meditate on Cakratuṇḍa, the vehicle of Śiva. May that bull, Nandī (*dharma*), illumine us.

16. *Ṣaṇmukha-Gāyatrī*

Oṃ. Tatpuruṣāya vidmahe
Mahāsenāya dhīmahi/
Tanno Ṣaṇmukhaḥ pracodayāt//

May we realize that *Tatpuruṣa,* the Cosmic Person. Let us meditate on that Mahāsena, the commander-in-chief of celestials and may that Ṣaṇmukha, the six-faced god (Subrahmaṇya, the son of Śiva), illumine us.

17. *Candra-Gāyatrī*

Oṃ. Kṣīraputrāya vidmahe
Amṛtatattvāya dhīmahi/
Tanno Candraḥ pracodayāt//

May we realize that son of ocean of milk. Let us meditate on that principle of nectar. May that Candra, the presiding deity over the moon, illumine us.

18. *Yama-Gāyatrī*

Oṃ. Sūryaputrāya vidmahe
Mahākālāya dhīmahi/
Tanno Yamaḥ pracodayāt//

May we realize that son of sun-god. Let us meditate on that great time, that ends everything. May that Yama, the god of death, illumine us.

19. *Pṛthvī-Gāyatrī*

Oṃ. Pṛthvī-devyai vidmahe
Sahasramūrtyai dhīmahi/
Tanno Pṛthvī pracodayāt//

May we realize Prithvī-Devī, the Mother Earth. Let us meditate on her thousand aspects as Sahasramūrti. May Pṛthvī, the Mother Earth, illumine us.

20. *Hayagrīva-Gāyatrī*

Oṃ. Vāṇīśvarāya vidmahe
Hayagrīvāya dhīmahi/
Tanno Hayagrīvaḥ pracodayāt//

May we realize that Vāṇīśvara, who blesses us with vocabulary. Let us meditate on Hayagrīva, the horse-faced god. May Hayagrīva the munificent Lord illumine us.

Oṃ. Śāntiḥ Śāntiḥ Śāntiḥ